The Battle of Britain Memorial Flight

First published as Battle of Britain Memorial Flight in 2018
This expanded edition published in 2023
by Tempest Books
an imprint of Mortons Books Ltd.
Media Centre Morton Way
Horncastle LN9 6JR
www.mortonsbooks.co.uk
Copyright © Tempest Books, 2023

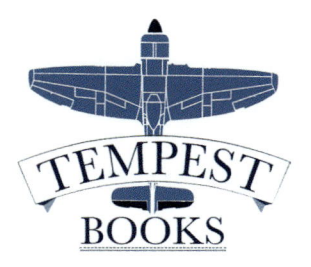

Tempest Books

All rights reserved. No part of this publication may be reproduced or transmitted in any form or by any means, electronic or mechanical including photocopying, recording, or any information storage retrieval system without prior permission in writing from the publisher.
ISBN 978-1-911658-45-0
Typeset by Chris Sandham-Bailey
Thanks: Thank you to everyone who has kindly provided photographs. Wherever possible individual credit has been given. Special thanks go to Lisa Harding, David Gait, Peter Arnold for Spitfire histories and photographs, a special thank you to Clive Rowley, Suggs, Disco and the BBMF for allowing access to the collection.
Heather, Erin & Noah for their support.

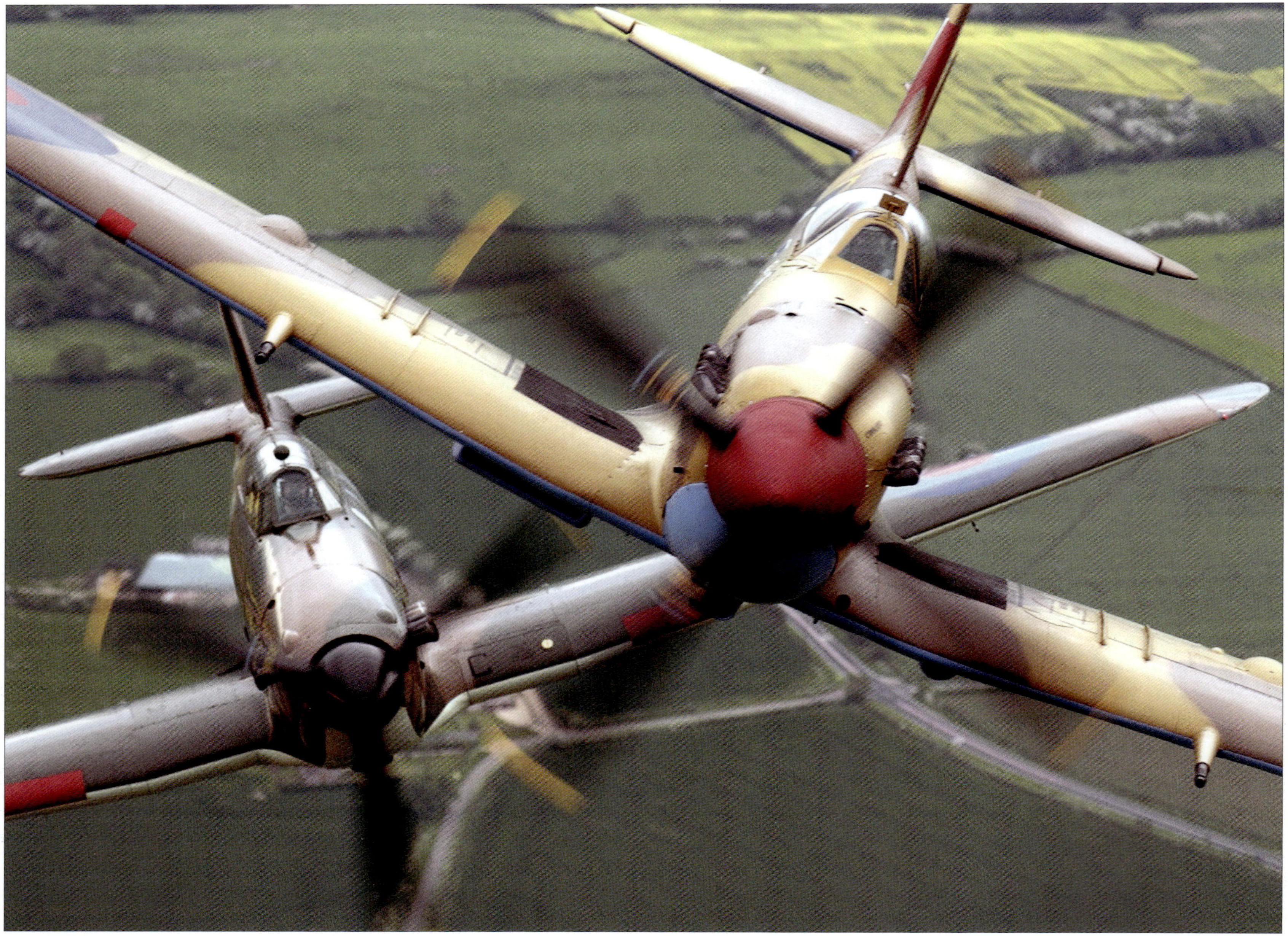

CONTENTS

INTRODUCTION	6
BRIEF HISTORY OF THE BBMF	8
SPITFIRE MK.IIA P7350	12
SPITFIRE MK.VB AB910	40
SPITFIRE LF.IXE MK356	76
SPITFIRE MK.XVIE TE311	98
SPITFIRE PR MK.XIX PM631	122
SPITFIRE PR MK.XIX PS915	146
HURRICANE MK.IIC LF363	170
HURRICANE MK.IIC PZ865	198
LANCASTER PA474	222
DAKOTA ZA947	250
CHIPMUNKS	270
BBMF AIRCRAFT TIMELINE	296

INTRODUCTION

By Squadron Leader Mark Sugden, Officer Commanding RAF Battle of Britain Memorial Flight

As the Officer Commanding the Battle of Britain Memorial Flight, I am humbled by the prestigious aircraft that we are fortunate enough to be custodians of. Whilst the aircraft themselves are some of the most recognisable in the history of the Royal Air Force and our aviation heritage, it is the human endeavour they represent that lies at the heart of what BBMF stands for. We are a living memorial to those who have served and sacrificed in the service of our great nation, and we are dedicated to keeping their memory alive.

As the Officer Commanding, one of the many "perks" of the job is to choose the livery of our aircraft. Every scheme that our aircraft proudly wear is authentic to the type and mark of aircraft and is chosen after extensive research. Each depicts a squadron, a pilot, or story that needs to be told and remembered. Importantly our aircraft display the markings of countries from across the Commonwealth, who aided in turning the tide against a regime that threatened our very way of life and existence.

To fly any of our aircraft and to become part of its history is an incredible honour, and is without doubt the defining moment of my RAF career. I am often asked what it is like to fly such iconic aircraft. The experience transcends words. To be in a cockpit that has witnessed such bravery, heroism and courage is almost impossible to describe.

Having been formed at Biggin Hill in 1957, the BBMF is now in its 66th year and is a household name, indeed a national treasure. We appear at occasions of state, air shows and public

INTRODUCTION

events every summer and are seen by millions of people across the globe. The small, but passionate BBMF team work tirelessly to preserve our incredible aircraft and keep them in flying condition. In addition to commemorating our past, we strive to celebrate and promote the present, and inspire future generations.

I am hugely grateful to Chris Sandham-Bailey for producing such a detailed account and illustration of our aircraft's history and the stories they have told over the years, and will continue to tell. I hope next time you look skywards and marvel at the unrivalled sight and sound of a BBMF aircraft, you will appreciate even more the significance of the aircraft and of course those it represents.

Lest We Forget

PA474 Flying into the dusk. CROWN COPYRIGHT

The 'Boss' with AB910. SQN LDR MARK SUGDEN

HISTORY OF THE BATTLE OF BRITAIN MEMORIAL FLIGHT IN PROFILE

The BBMF can trace its origins back to the Historical Air Flight, which was formed at Biggin Hill in July 1957 with the arrival of three Spitfire PR.XIXs on the 11th of that month. These were PM631, PS835 and PS915. All three are still flying, although PS835 was sold to raise funds for the restoration of Hurricane LF363 in 1994.

In the immediate post-war years there was a surplus of military aircraft that required disposal. Many were relegated to secondary roles, such as training or as target tugs, but the majority headed to the scrapyard for recycling. Where some types are concerned, such as the Short Stirling or Westland Whirlwind, no examples survived and of others, such as the Bristol Beaufort and Handley Page Halifax, only very few now remain in museums.

Just ten years after the war there was only one airworthy Hurricane. Most of those who held senior rank within the RAF at that time had fought during the war and were concerned about historical aircraft being lost, especially the Hurricane and Spitfire. Many felt that at least some of these aircraft should be preserved as a tribute to the fighter pilots of the war and specifically the Battle of Britain. One man who firmly held this opinion was Wing Commander Peter Thompson, the station commander at Biggin Hill during the 1950s.

Thompson joined the RAF Volunteer Reserve in 1938 following the Munich Crisis and had become a trainee pilot just after the outbreak of war in September 1939. He flew Hurricanes during the Battle of Britain with 32 and 605 Squadrons, followed by a posting to Malta. Thompson also spent time in the Western Desert with the Spitfire and finished the war commanding 129 Sqn, flying Mustangs. During 1955 Thompson was posted to Biggin Hill as a wing commander and the next year he became station commander. It was not long after this that he 'rescued' Hurricane LF363, which had been somewhat neglected in the post-war years, but had since been restored by Hawker. Thompson personally flew it to Biggin Hill on June 28, 1956, and was involved in the Battle of Britain flypast that September. Concurrently, he also sought and was granted permission to form the Historic Aircraft Flight, although no official support or funding would be provided.

The following year the Temperature and Humidity Monitoring Flight based at Woodvale decided to retire its three Spitfire PR.XIXs, so they were allocated to the HAF. The aircraft were flown to Biggin Hill by Thompson, Gp Capt 'Johnny' Johnson and Gp Capt James Rankin. For the ferry flight they had an escort of Hunters and Javelins. The route was supposed to take in Duxford before going on to Biggin Hill on June 12, but due to technical issues two of the Spitfires went unserviceable and the flight was delayed until July 11, 1957. Upon arrival there was an official delegation, including Air Officer Commanding-in-Chief of Fighter Command, Air Marshal Sir Thomas Pike, and such was the level of public interest that the flight received national press coverage.

Although four aircraft had been saved, there remained dissenting voices from among those former fighter pilots who had fought in the Battle of Britain. They felt it would be better to preserve a Spitfire variant that had fought in the battle or, at the very least, had carried guns. While attending the Royal Tournament of 1957, Thompson saw a Mk.XVI, TE330, being used in the show and made a formal application for it to join the HAF. So, on September 15, TE330 and LF363 took part in the Battle of Britain flypast over Westminster Abbey. PS853 departed the flight on November 8 and was to fly in simulated combat at Binbrook with the Lightnings when it was thought the latter would have to develop techniques to engage Indonesian P-51D Mustangs in Malaysia.

The next year was a testing time for the fledgling flight. In February Thompson was posted away from Biggin Hill following the announcement of its imminent closure as an operational RAF station. This coincided with the HAF being officially renamed the Battle of Britain Flight and at the end of the month, the arrival of two more Royal Tournament attendees, Mk.XVI TE476 and SL574, both of which were restored to flying condition.

As the station closed it was decided to move the aircraft to North Weald, the actual move taking place on May 16. Fortunately, the station commander there was Gp Capt Sutton, who had flown LF363 during the flypast over London and was an advocate for the flight. Two Spitfires were then lost in quick succession, the PR.XIX PS853 went to West Raynham as a gate guardian in March just after the move. It was also announced that TE330 would be given to the USAF Academy as a gift, the handover taking place on July 14, 1958. North Weald was closed during the same month that TE330 departed, so for the second time in a few months the flight was required to relocate, this time to Martlesham Heath, where it managed to last three years before yet

The BBMF Hangar at Coningsby. AUTHOR

another station closure and move. While at Martlesham Heath, two of the Mk.XVIs left the flight. On May 28, 1959, SL574 suffered damage during a wheels-up landing. Then, having been repaired, it once again made a forced landing on September 20. Taking part in a flypast over London, SL574 was flown by AVM Maguire and while still over the capital the engine failed and he was forced to land on a cricket pitch in Bromley. Fortunately, it was during a break in play, but the wings did take out one of the sets of stumps. TE476 had been damaged during a landing accident only 10 days before at Martlesham Heath and both became gate guardians again.

PS915 had departed for static display as well, although it returned to the flight eventually, so the only two airworthy fighters were one Hurricane and one Spitfire. This made the move to Horsham St Faith quite straightforward on November 3, 1961, when yet another station was closed.

Having had a dismal few years that threatened the very existence of the flight, things were to change once it had moved to Coltishall on April 1, 1963, as the result of Horsham St Faith closing. The flight was bolstered by the return of PS853 in April 1964 and the fighters were joined by the D-Day veteran Spitfire Vb AB910 in September 1965. It was donated by Vickers Armstrong, delivered by Jeffery Quill and has remained with the flight ever since. In 1968, work commenced on the Battle of Britain film and all available aircraft were called upon for use in it, including those at Coltishall. They were all painted to represent early war aircraft and had a number of temporary serials and codes applied. Many of those that appeared had been purchased by Spitfire Productions Ltd and with the work completed, the aircraft had to be disposed of. This included Battle of Britain veteran Spitfire Mk.IIa P7350, which was given to the flight.

Although the flight had so far been supported and officially recognised, 1969 saw a change in its status. An agreement formally establishing it as the Battle of Britain Memorial Flight was sent by AM Sir Thomas Prickett at Whitehall to ACM Sir Dennis Spotswood, Air Officer Commanding-in-Chief, Headquarters Strike Command, on April 1. The letter also mentions that Waddington's Lancaster PA474 should also be considered for the BBMF, granting it a stay of execution and allowing for restoration work to be completed. The name was therefore changed to the Battle of Britain Memorial Flight on June 1, 1969.

The BBMF once more expanded when Hawker's chief test pilot Duncan Simpson delivered Hurricane Mk.IIc PZ865 to Coltishall on March 29, 1972. The company managing director, Sir John Lidbury, had originally promised the last Hurricane constructed, a significant and historical airframe, to the RAF Museum, but Simpson pushed for it to remain airworthy and with permission granted he took the initiative to deliver PZ865 before anyone changed their mind.

One year later, on November 20, 1973, Lancaster B.I PA474 left Waddington and bomber county for Norfolk and Coltishall in a move that would prove to be only short term, because the BBMF then relocated to Coningsby in March 1976.

Some believed the return of the Lancaster to Lincolnshire was the primary reason for the move, but Coningsby was actually in a stronger position to care for the enlarged fleet and could provide a dedicated hangar. Space had already been at a premium for Coltishall and with another Jaguar squadron forming at the station, there would be no room for the BBMF. Coningsby is also geographically more central, reducing the number of precious flying hours required to transition to display locations across the country. The aircraft arrived at their new station on March 1, 1976, and have remained there to date.

AB910 was put out of action for a couple of years in 1978 following a ground taxiing accident on August 21 at Bex, Switzerland. The head-on collision resulted in AB910 being rebuilt and returning to the air in 1981. PR.XIX PS853 was grounded in 1980 and did not fly again until fitted with a new and slightly larger Griffon 58 engine, the test flight taking place on July 20, 1989.

Chipmunk WK518 arrived in April 1983, joining Chipmunk T.10 WP855 (which had been added to the flight in 1975 while still at Coltishall) and serving multiple roles, familiarising pilots with tail draggers, ferrying crew and providing reconnaissance information for potential display locations. While the Chipmunks were suitable for one or two and carrying small parts, a larger transport aircraft was required for the supernumerary fleet. This was addressed in May 1985 when Devon C.1 VP981 was acquired and remained the primary transport until the arrival of the Dakota.

The first post-restoration flight for Spitfire PR.XIX PS915 was made on November 20, 1986. It had received a modified Griffon 58 engine and was signed off and returned to Coningsby on April 7, 1987. Chipmunk WP855 left the BBMF for 1 Air Experience Flight and there was a several year wait for a replacement.

After a few relatively uneventful years the BBMF suffered another tragedy with the loss of Hurricane Mk.IIc LF363 on September 11, 1991. While flying to Jersey with a full fuel load, the engine cut out during an emergency approach to Wittering and LF363 caught fire. After an extensive rebuild it eventually flew again in September 1998. LF363 would suffer a minor accident again on June 6, 2004, when the starboard undercarriage failed. This was much quicker to repair than the previous accident, however.

A replacement for the Devon arrived in March 1993 with the delivery of Dakota ZA947, which was originally going to be put up for disposal until RAF Strike Command acquired it and, following a repaint in wartime markings at Marham, it was delivered to Coningsby. The Devon remained with the flight until 1998 when it was sold to Air Atlantique. Between the arrival of the Dakota and departure of the Devon there were further aircraft movements. Spitfire PR.XIX PS853 was sold to fund the complete rebuild of LF363 on February 17, 1995 and the BBMF also gained another Chipmunk WG486, which was delivered to the flight the same year.

Ironically, the BBMF had to rely on the Luftwaffe for assistance on May 6, 2009, when the Lancaster was stranded at Schiphol, Amsterdam requiring an engine replacement following number four going unserviceable. Normally under such circumstances the Dakota would have ferried the engine, but a Luftwaffe C-160 was used for the role instead.

Further problems were to beset the BBMF on May 7, 2015, when the Lancaster suffered an engine fire during a training flight. Fortunately, it was able to return to Coningsby and the damage was kept to a minimum.

Two years later, on August 16, 2017, all the Merlin engine aircraft were grounded as a precaution following an inspection of one of the Hurricanes that resulted in traces of metal being found in an oil sample. This was then sent away for analysis. It was found that there was abnormal wear to the pinion gear in the reduction gearbox and by September 9 the Lancaster was flying again, having had its gearboxes externally inspected.

Although the BBMF was originally founded to remember the pilots of the Battle of Britain and still retains this in its name, it has since come to represent all those pilots who flew with the RAF and associated nations during and after the Second World War.

P7350. Author

SUPERMARINE SPITFIRE Mk.IIa P7350

Spitfire Mk.IIa P7350 is special even among the Spitfires still flying. It was the 14th of 11,939 built at the Castle Bromwich site and is the only currently airworthy example that was involved in combat during the Battle of Britain.

Under Lord Nuffield the factory at Castle Bromwich failed to produce a single Spitfire but, following the intervention of Lord Beaverbrook, a slow build-up of construction took place.

In July 1940 the first 23 were completed. Among these early examples was P7350, although it did not fly until the following month when taken for an air test by Alex Henshaw.

It was initially sent to 6 Maintenance Unit at Brize Norton, but when it was decided that 266 (Rhodesia) Squadron, based at Wittering, would replace its Mk.Is with the Mk.IIa, P7350 was included in the delivery on September 6 and received the code UT-O. The squadron had already seen heavy fighting in the south and had been moved to recover and re-equip, but during this time it still saw limited action.

Just over a month after receiving the Mk.IIa, 266 Sqn reverted to the Mk.I, transferring the newer Spitfires, including P7350, to 603 (City of Edinburgh) Squadron at Hornchurch on October 17, 1940. With fighting still very intense, P7350 only lasted a short time before being damaged in combat with Bf 109s and a crash landing on October 25 while being flown by Polish pilot PO Ludwig Martel. Despite the wheels-up landing it was recovered and was at 1 Civilian Repair Unit at Cowley, Oxfordshire, by the end of the month. The original bullet holes in the port wing gained from the combat remained patched up until a major service in 2008.

Having been repaired, P7350 was placed in storage, probably due to the respite from fighting during the winter and increase in Spitfire production, but 616 (South Yorkshire) Squadron received it while at Tangmere on March 18, 1941, for a few weeks until it was passed over to 64 Squadron at Hornchurch on April 10.

UO-T 266 SQUADRON, AUGUST-OCTOBER 1940 & 1989

It stayed with 64 Sqn for several months until it was sent to Prestwick, where Scottish Aviation undertook a major overhaul in August. This was the last time that P7350 served with a front-line squadron as it spent the remaining war years in secondary roles, first at the Central Gunnery School, Sutton Bridge, and then, following an accident on February 4, 1943, it was repaired and flown by 57 Operational Training Unit, Eshott. It was damaged again when another Spitfire taxied into it on April 22, 1944. Following repairs it was placed in storage before being sold as scrap on July 8, 1948 for the princely sum of £25.

Fortunately, instead of destroying P7350, the new owners, Messrs John Dale Ltd, understood the provenance of the Battle of Britain veteran and donated it to the RAF Colerne Collection as a static display. It remained there until March 1967 when it was purchased by Spitfire Productions Ltd and registered with the civilian code G-AWIJ, although the Ministry of Defence retained ultimate ownership with a view to using it for the planned Battle of Britain film. It was transported by road to Henlow and restored to flying condition. As one of the first Spitfires acquired for the film it received a new scheme, albeit without any codes or serial. While waiting for filming to commence it was one of three Spitfires used in the background of the opening scene for the 1968 film The Devil's Brigade.

As a flying example of an 'authentic' Battle of Britain Spitfire,

SUPERMARINE SPITFIRE Mk.IIa P7350

XT-W 603 SQUADRON, OCTOBER 1940

P7350 was used extensively during the filming and it wore a wide variety of codes and serials including; AI-A/E/S, BO-C/H, CD-B/C/G/H/M, DO-E/M & EI-C/Q along with the serials N3310, N3312, N3313, N3316, N3317, N3321, N3324 and N3329. With filming complete in November the Spitfires were disposed of but the historic provenance of P7350 was recognised again and it was presented to the BBMF, arriving at Coltishall on November 8, 1968, the then CO AVM George Black taking delivery.

The film markings and scheme had been removed and replaced with the code ZH-T of 266 Sqn, the unit that P7350 first served with — although the squadron did not introduce the ZH code letters until July 1942, long after P7350 had departed and been relegated to secondary duties.

The error was corrected in 1972 and the historically accurate UO was applied. The scheme remained until the winter of 1977/78 when, during an overhaul, it was completely repainted, not for the last time, in the markings of 19 Sqn, wearing the code QV-B, X4179. The squadron was the first to receive the Spitfire on August 4, 1938, while stationed at Duxford and fought throughout the Battle of Britain. There was another change of markings in 1982 with yet another Battle of Britain squadron being represented, SH-D of 64 Sqn. At the outbreak of war the squadron was operating the Blenheim IF but was flying the Spitfire Mk.I throughout the summer of 1940, not converting to the Mk.II until the following year. This scheme lasted until 1985 when P7350 was painted in the markings of P7666

SH-D 64 SQUADRON, APRIL 1941 & 1982

EB-Z 'Observer Corps', 41 Sqn. It was quite common during the war for aircraft to be bought with funds raised by wealthy individuals, groups or companies and one such case was the Observer Corps (later Royal Observer Corps). Its members raised £5,000 for Spitfire P7666.

The Observer Corps went on to raise enough money for a second Spitfire, P7837, QJ-B which went to 616 Sqn. 41 Sqn took delivery of P7666 on November 21, 1940, where it remained until the following February when, having been converted to a Mk.Vb, it was allocated to 54 Sqn. Two months later, on April 20, it was being flown by P/O Stokoe when he was shot down over the channel by a Bf 109. The Spitfire was lost but Stokoe was picked up by Air Sea Rescue.

To commemorate the 50th anniversary of the Battle of Britain P7350 returned to its wartime markings of 266 Sqn, UO-T, repainted for the 1989 and 1990 display seasons. It went back to the paint shop at the end of 1990 to receive the markings of 65 Sqn's YT-F, a 1941 scheme from the period when the squadron was equipped with the Mk.IIa and Mk.IIb, having previously had the Mk.I during the Battle of Britain. While photos of the original YT-F have part of the serial obscured, it was probably P7697 that was flown by Sgt W Kay when it was shot down by a Bf 109 just off Dunkirk on August 21, 1941, and Kay was killed. While flying as YT-F P7350 suffered an engine failure and during the forced landing it overran the runway, nosing over on July 29, 1992.

SUPERMARINE SPITFIRE Mk.IIa P7350

RAF COLERNE COLLECTION, CIRCA 1965

The YT-F scheme only lasted two years when in 1994 it was changed to RN-S, a Mk.IIa that was first flown by 72 Sqn on January 12, 1971, purchased with funds raised by the *Belfast Telegraph*. P7832 was named 'Enniskillen' and bore the legend 'Belfast Telegraph Spitfire Fund' on both sides. It went on to serve with 74 & 610 squadrons and then, having survived combat, it was passed to 61 Operational Training Unit. P7832 was eventually struck off charge in June 1945.

Yet another presentation Spitfire was chosen for the 1997 scheme, P8509 'The Old Lady' was donated by the Bank of England with staff raising funds and received by 277 Sqn on December 21, 1942, when the code BA-Y was applied. 277 Sqn was primarily an Air Sea Rescue squadron flying a mix of Walrus and Lysander, the former being used to pick up aircrew. The Lysander was used for spotting but the squadron also used Defiants and Spitfires for this role, including P8509.

During early 1999, P7350's scheme was changed to that of L1067 XT-D of 603 (City of Edinburgh) Squadron. It bore the name of the race horse 'Blue Peter' in red on the port side. L1067 was delivered to the RAF on July 26, 1939, and held at 27 MU until just after the outbreak of war when it was delivered to the squadron on September 16, while being flown by Sqn Ldr G Denholm, the squadron CO on August 30, 1940, when he engaged some Bf 110s over Deal. Receiving hits, Denholm bailed out and L1067 crashed at Hope Farm, Snargate, Kent. Only two days later Denholm was flying again and damaged

ZH 266 SQUADRON, EARLY 1966

a Bf 109. He finished the war with six kills (four destroyed and four shared), three probables, one shared probable and five damaged. During May 2006 the scheme was temporarily changed to XT-W which it is thought was the original code letter worn by P7350 when it was first with the squadron.

P7350 maintained its link with 603 Sqn when in 2007 it was painted in the markings of L1020 XT-L, flown by Basil Gerald 'Stapme' Stapleton when he claimed a Me 109 E as a probable on August 31, 1940. A week after this action L1020 was being flown by P/O P Cardell when it was damaged during an encounter with some Bf 109s on September 6 and crash landed near Ilford, Essex. Stapleton was rested after the Battle of Britain and then volunteered to fly Hurricanes with North Atlantic convoys. The Hurricanes were aging airframes that were catapult launched from the ships and because they could not be recovered they would be ditched and the pilot hopefully picked up by the convoy. After four uneventful trips he returned to the UK flying Hurricanes as bomber escorts. In August 1944 Stapleton found himself in charge of 247 Sqn flying Typhoons in France. By the time he was made a POW as the result of a forced landing behind German lines on December 23, 1944, he had claimed six enemy aircraft destroyed, two shared destroyed, eight probably destroyed and two damaged. During late 2008 and 2009, P7350 was given a comprehensive overhaul by the Aircraft Restoration

SUPERMARINE SPITFIRE Mk.IIa P7350

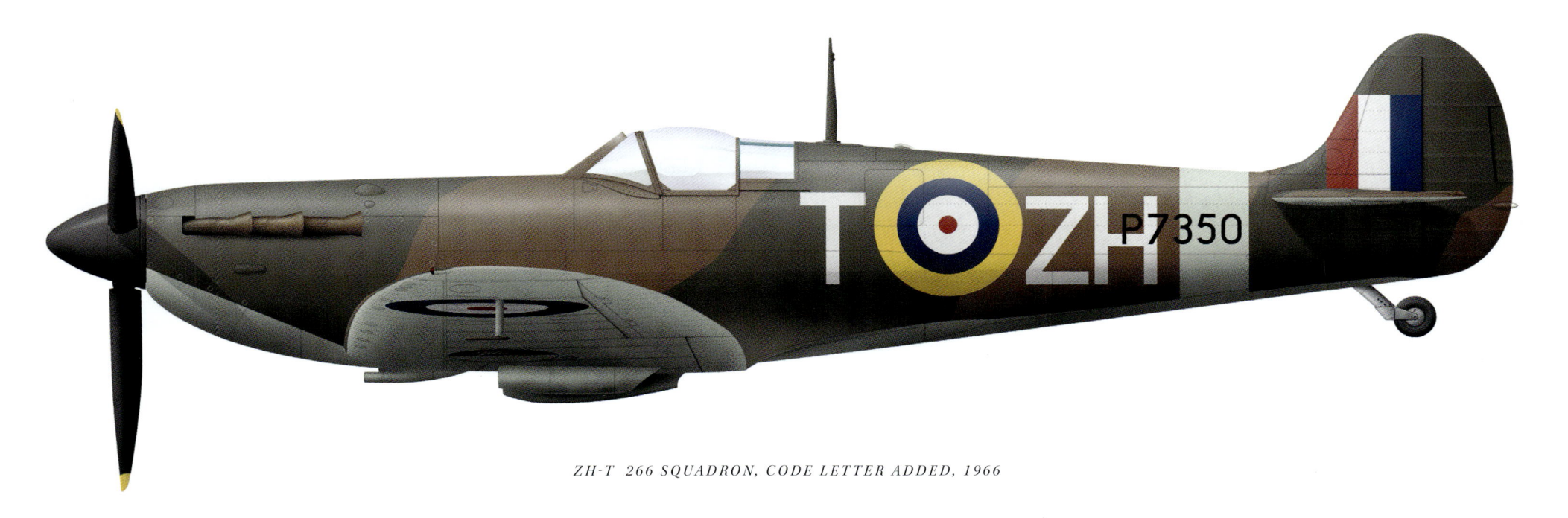

ZH-T 266 SQUADRON, CODE LETTER ADDED, 1966

Company at Duxford, returning to the air on September 16, 2009. As is standard practice the markings were changed to those of Geoffrey Wellum's 92 Sqn Spitfire Mk.Ia K9998, QJ-K. Wellum's exploits during the Battle of Britain were covered in his autobiography First Light. In February 1942 he became a flight commander with 65 Sqn and in August that year he was posted to 145 Sqn in Malta, flying a Spitfire off the deck of *HMS Furious*. Returning from Malta in 1943, he became a test pilot for the Typhoon. K9998 had already served with 504 and 603 Squadrons before arriving at 92 Sqn. It was then used by various OTUs until it crash landed at Hawarden on August 26, 1941.

Spitfire Mk.Ia N3162 EB-G of 41 Sqn was the chosen scheme for P7350 and was worn from 2011 to 2017. N3162 was flown by Eric Lock who was at the controls on September 5, 1940, the day he became an ace by shooting down two He 111s, two Bf 109 Es and a further Bf 109 E claimed as a probable, all during only his second encounter with the Luftwaffe. Lock was lost the following year when, on August 3, during a patrol near Pas-de-Calais, he was seen by his wingman preparing to attack ground targets. Neither he nor his aircraft were found. By the time of this action he had amassed 26 confirmed kills.

During 2017 P7350 wore temporary markings, once again Wellum's QJ-G code was on the port side and Ken Wilkinson's QV-A on the starboard side. Wilkinson was also a participant in the Battle of Britain, joining 616 Sqn in October 1940 for a very brief period as he was posted to 19 Sqn on the 17th. During one later interview he said:

19

THE DEVIL'S BRIGADE FILM, 1967

"I didn't carry any lucky charms, but I did wear a pair of my wife's knickers around my neck." Wilkinson died aged 99 on July 31, 2017.

Yet another Battle of Britain Spitfire was represented when Al Deere's Kiwi III was unveiled for the 2018 display season. Deere, born in Auckland, New Zealand, was posted to 54 Sqn before the war in September 1938 while the squadron was still flying Gladiators, but converted to Spitfires the following spring. Before Kiwi III, Deere had previously flown Kiwi, N3180, a Mk.Ia, which he crash landed on the beach between Ostend and Dunkirk during the evacuation on May 28, 1940, having been shot down.

This was followed by Kiwi II, P9390, also a Mk.Ia, which he used almost exclusively, but on July 7, 1940, it was being flown by P/O Jack Coleman, who was shot down and crashed near Deal. Two days later R6895 was one of two Spitfires delivered to 54 Sqn as replacements and Deere laid claim to it, applying Kiwi III and the emblem of the diminutive flightless bird on both sides in keeping with his last two planes.

On July 11 Deere took his new Spitfire up for the first time and over the course of the month he flew it a total of 38 times, 23 of those being operational flights. At the end of the month the squadron was rested for a week, retiring to Catterick and it was here that Deere made a wheels-up landing in R6895. Deere flew

SUPERMARINE SPITFIRE Mk.IIa P7350

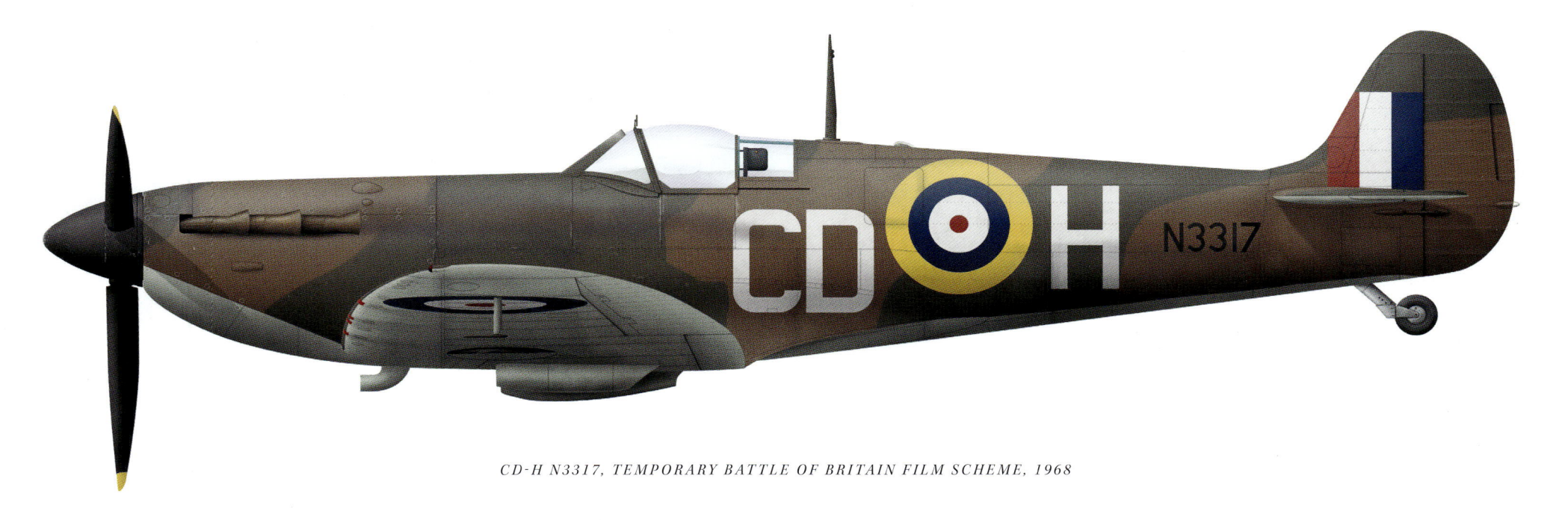

CD-H N3317, TEMPORARY BATTLE OF BRITAIN FILM SCHEME, 1968

a replacement while it was being repaired and on one occasion he was attacked by some Bf 109s that managed to hit the Spitfire.

Amazingly, despite the damage to the cockpit and his watch face being shot off, Deere was unharmed and proceeded to bail out, fracturing his wrist in the process as it caught the tail plane. Kiwi III was returned to the squadron and Deere continued to fly it until August 31 when it was blown up. The squadron was attempting to take off during a raid on Hornchurch and three aircraft were lost; Deere's Spitfire was flipped upside down and lost a wing in the process. Once again though, it was repaired and served with 58 OTU until retired in August 1944.

During the first few months of 1941 Deere was rested from front line duties while he trained new pilots but he was posted to 602 Sqn as flight commander in May 1941 and two months later he took over as the squadron OC. He later became Biggin Hill Wing Leader and went on to command the Fighter Wing of the Central Gunnery School. Although posted to a staff job, he took command of a Free French Fighter Wing in time for D-Day. He finished the war with 22 kills, 10 probables and 18 damaged.

Spitfire Mk.IIa P7350 is the oldest aircraft operated by the BBMF and the only one to have actually seen action in the Battle of Britain. Were it not for the generosity of the film-makers in 1968, the flight would not have this most fitting of tributes to the battle to which it owes its name.

BATTLE OF BRITAIN MEMORIAL FLIGHT IN PROFILE

DO-M, POST BATTLE OF BRITAIN FILM, 1968

ZH-T 266 SQUADRON, 1969

22

SUPERMARINE SPITFIRE Mk.IIa P7350

QV-B 19 SQUADRON, REPRESENTING X4179, 1977

EB-Z 'OBSERVER CORPS' 41 SQUADRON, REPRESENTING P7666, 1985

BATTLE OF BRITAIN MEMORIAL FLIGHT IN PROFILE

YT-F 65 SQUADRON, REPRESENTING P7697, 1991

RN-S 'ENNISKILLEN/BELFAST TELEGRAPH SPITFIRE FUND' 72 SQUADRON, REPRESENTING P7832, 1994

SUPERMARINE SPITFIRE Mk.IIa P7350

BA-Y 'THE OLD LADY' 227 SQUADRON, REPRESENTING P8509, 1997

XT-D 'BLUE PETER' 603 SQUADRON, REPRESENTING L1607, 1999

BATTLE OF BRITAIN MEMORIAL FLIGHT IN PROFILE

XT-L 603 SQUADRON, REPRESENTING L1020, 2007

QJ-K 92 SQUADRON, REPRESENTING K9998, 2009

SUPERMARINE SPITFIRE Mk.IIa P7350

EB-G 41 SQUADRON, REPRESENTING N3162, 2012

QJ-G 92 SQUADRON, 2017

BATTLE OF BRITAIN MEMORIAL FLIGHT IN PROFILE

KL-B 'KIWI III' 54 SQUADRON, REPRESENTING R6981, 2018

SUPERMARINE SPITFIRE Mk.IIa P7350

BATTLE OF BRITAIN MEMORIAL FLIGHT IN PROFILE

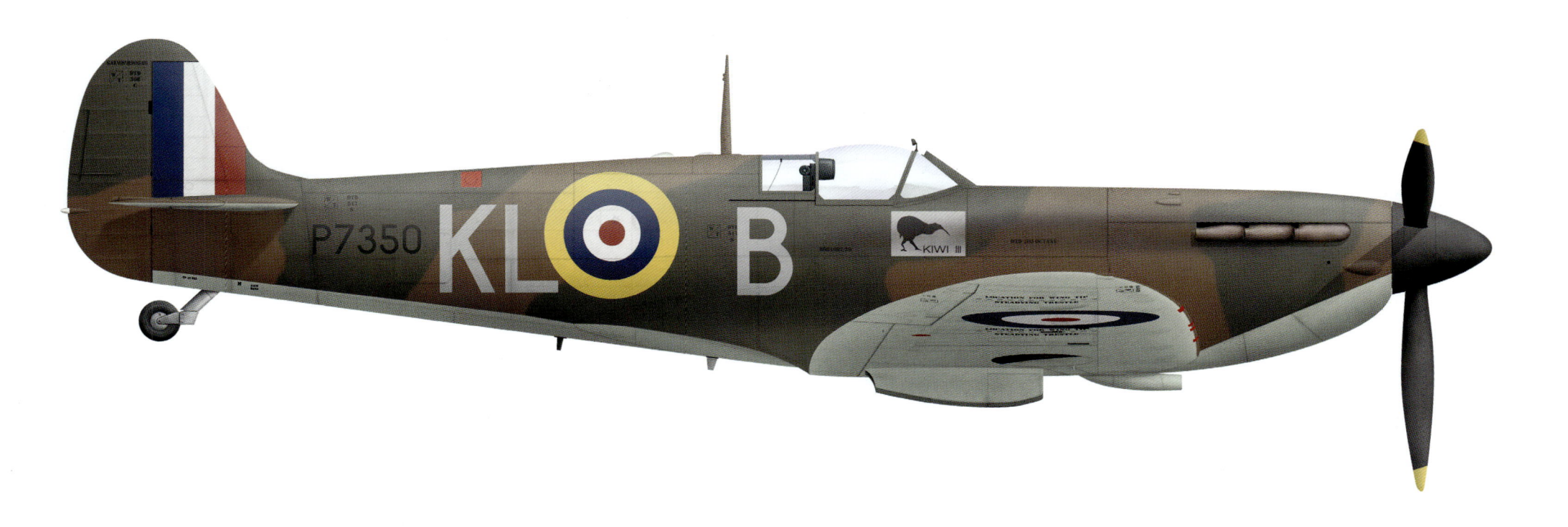

SUPERMARINE SPITFIRE Mk.IIa P7350

P7350 in a Light Grey and Dark Green scheme at Colerne with Heinkel He 162 in the background. RON CRANHAM, PETER ARNOLD COLLECTION

P7350 having received a first coat of paint circa 1963. DAVID WELCH

P7350 following the completion of filming Battle of Britain with temporary code applied at Coltishall, 1968. PETER ARNOLD COLLECTION

P7350 painted as ZH of 226 Squadron prior to addition of the T, early 1966. JAMES KIGHTLY COLLECTION

SUPERMARINE SPITFIRE Mk.IIa P7350

Taxiing in front of Lightnings of 29 & 111 squadrons at Wattisham. MARK TAYLOR

BATTLE OF BRITAIN MEMORIAL FLIGHT IN PROFILE

P7350 with later ZH-T scheme, September 1961. Ron Cranham, Peter Arnold Collection

Wearing the same scheme as when it first entered service with 266 squadron, circa 1990. BAe Systems

QV-B scheme of 19 squadron following a display at Duxford, 1978. David Welch

'Observer Corps' presentation Spitfire scheme, 1985. San Diego Air & Space Museum

34

XT-D with lowered flaps coming into land. JAMES KIGHTLY COLLECTION

BA-Y 'The Old Lady' at Duxford for the 60th anniversary of the Spitfire, 3 May 1998. LES CHATFIELD

P7350 with AB910 and Hurricane PZ865 at Fairford, 1997. IAN POWELL

P7350 following a forced landing due to engine failure at Chivenor, 1992. AUTHOR

P7350 in formation with Lancaster PA474 and Spitfire PM631 at Duxford, 2012. AUTHOR

SUPERMARINE SPITFIRE Mk.IIa P7350

Taxiing at RIAT in July 2011. RONNIE MACDONALD

P7350 and Hurricane LF363 Breaking. LISA HARDING

P7350 with AB910 and Hurricane PZ865 at Fairford, 1997. IAN POWELL

Taxiing with PS915. ROB MONFEA

37

Starting up at Coningsby. LISA HARDING

Flypast. Lisa Harding

On jacks with the undercarriage removed during winter service. AUTHOR

SUPERMARINE SPITFIRE MK.Vb AB910

With a colourful history to say the least, AB910 is a combat veteran and one of the Flight's mainstays.

Allocated the construction number CBAF1061, AB910 was built at Castle Bromwich and completed in July 1941. It was handed to the RAF and delivered to 222 (Natal) Squadron at RAF North Weald, Essex, on August 22 that year. Given the code ZD-C, it was first used operationally on August 26 when P/O Ramsey flew it during a patrol off Goodwin Sands. Ramsey was the only pilot to use AB910 during its time with 222 Sqn, flying a total of six missions before it was damaged during a landing accident on August 31 following a patrol providing cover for the Royal Navy.

Having been repaired at Hamble by Air Service Training it was transferred to 37 Maintenance Unit at Burtonwood and held until it was allocated to 130 Squadron based at RAF Perranporth, Cornwall and resumed combat operations on December 13. Once again AB910 had a short stay, lasting only a couple of weeks before it was damaged. The squadron code was LE but it is unknown what letter AB910 received.

During the 18 days with 130 Squadron it flew 12 missions and the most notable of these were two trips to Brest during Operation Veracity, part of an ongoing series of raids over the winter on the German battleships *Scharnhorst* and *Gneisenau*, and the heavy cruiser *Prinz Eugen*. Veracity I took place on December 18 when the squadron, including AB910, provided fighter cover for a 121 bomber raid, comprising Vickers Wellingtons, Handley Page Hampdens and Armstrong Whitworth Whitleys.

On December 30 a smaller force made up of Halifaxes returned to Brest with AB910 flying escort once again and engaging 20 Bf 109s. This was the last action taken with 130 Sqn and it was not recorded what damage AB910 suffered, but it is on record as being sent to Westland's factory in Yeovil for repairs.

MD-E 133 EAGLE SQUADRON, JUNE-JULY 1942, 1991 & 2013

AB910 was once again airworthy on March 28, 1942, and dispatched on April 8 to 6 MU, Brize Norton, where it remained in storage until it was allocated to 133 (Eagle) Squadron, Biggin Hill on June 13. The squadron was one of three that was made up of American pilots who wanted to fight before the US had entered the war. AB910 saw extensive action including four sorties on August 18 when the RAF attempted to draw out and engage the Luftwaffe during Operation Jubilee, the Allied raid on Dieppe. During one flight, F/O E Doorly damaged a Do 217. Then later in the day F/Sgt R Alexander destroyed a Do 217.

The next day was the last time AB910 was operational with 133 Sqn. It continued to be used for training but the pilots of 133 Sqn were due to be integrated into the US Army Air Force with the renaming of the squadron as the 336th Fighter Squadron of the 4th Fighter Group and the Spitfire was sent to 242 Squadron, RAF Digby, Lincolnshire. The squadron was due to relocate to the Middle East so they only flew training missions during this period. As the personnel shipped out, AB910 was once again placed into storage in the care of 12 MU at Kirkbride on November 12. It remained here for several months until it returned to RAF Digby and 416 Squadron RCAF in July 1943, with the squadron code DN. From then on AB910 had what could be considered a charmed life, seeing continuous active service for just over a year following an engine change days after joining the squadron.

SUPERMARINE SPITFIRE MK.Vb AB910

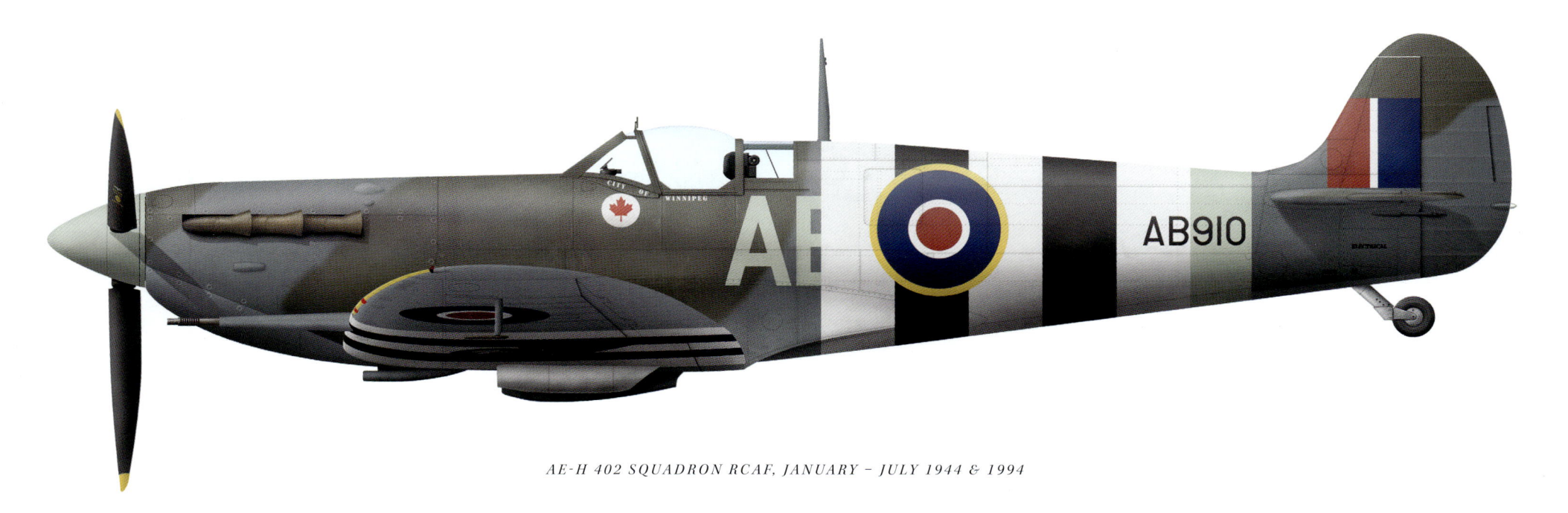

AE-H 402 SQUADRON RCAF, JANUARY – JULY 1944 & 1994

In January 1944 the squadron converted to the Spitfire Mk.IX and the existing aircraft were taken over by 402 City of Winnipeg Squadron RCAF, with AB910 arriving at Digby, where the squadron was based on February 1, 1944. The code AE-H was applied and the squadron moved south to commence operations on March 1, when it was flown for the first time by Sqn Ldr G W Northcott. The squadron conducted a roadstead with some Beaufighters, a low level attack on shipping in a harbour. Northcott continued to fly AB910 in a combination of escort and attack missions until the end of May.

AB910 was only flown twice on D-Day, the first time by F/O G B Lawson when the aircraft took off at 09.45 and provided beachhead cover over the eastern area, landing at 12.15. The squadron then provided cover again in the late evening with P/O H C Nicholson as pilot for the two-hour flight, taking off at 22.00 and landing at 23.59. The squadron, including AB910, continued to fly extensively over Normandy throughout June.

With 402 Sqn RCAF following other squadrons and exchanging their Mk.Vs for Mk.IXs, AB910 was retired from operational flying and sent to 53 Operational Training Unit at Hibaldstow. The code was changed to MV-T for Trouble which was quite apt because on February 14, 1945, possibly the most unusual incident in AB910's long history occurred. It has long been the practice (continued to this day) on uneven surfaces and

MV-T 53 OPERATIONAL CONVERSION UNIT, 1945

in windy conditions to have a member of the ground crew sit on the tail to add extra weight and reduce the chances of a Spitfire tipping over on its nose.

At Hibaldstow the 'Rough Weather Procedure' as it was known was mandatory before all flights while a Spitfire was taxiing. It would then stop, allowing the ground crew to dismount before commencing the take-off run.

However, on this particular day LACW Margaret Ida Horton, a WAAF fitter, was not given the opportunity to dismount. She later said: "We had reached the runway intersecting the one actually in use, and I was waiting for the aircraft to slow up for me to slip down, when I suddenly realised that she was increasing speed. It was too late to jump off, so I flung myself across the fuselage and grasped the elevator on the port side in a vain effort to attract the pilot's attention. Even before I had given up the attempt the change of movement told me we were 'upstairs'. There was nothing to hold on to but the cut-away corner of the elevator into which I had inserted three fingers."

The pilot, Flt Lt Neil Cox DFC was unaware of his passenger throughout the flight but he was experiencing severe issues with the elevators. Cox managed to climb to 800ft, while completing a circuit he was informed by the tower to land immediately, having become aware of Horton's predicament. AB910 was brought in for a perfect landing and it is reported that Horton

SUPERMARINE SPITFIRE MK.Vb AB910

G-AISU IN ALL METAL WITH RED CODE, 1949

made a safe dismount and rather shakily lit a cigarette. In Cox's defence the aircraft controller had given him permission to take off without seeing his Spitfire or its unwitting passenger.

Soon after AB910 left 53 OTU for its last military posting for many years when it was transferred to 527 Sqn at Digby where it was used for radar calibration until it was retired on May 30, 1946, and put up for disposal. AB910 came under civilian ownership when it was purchased for £200 by Gp Capt Alan Wheeler with the intention of competing in post-war civilian races. Work was carried out by Vickers Swindon factory and initially AB910 was stripped of paint and the civil code G-AISU was applied in red on the fuselage. However, it was soon painted in Oxford Blue with gold cheatlines on the fuselage and the aircraft also had the armour window, cannon and aerial removed to reduce weight. A four-bladed propeller was also fitted to improve performance and it would be several decades before AB910 returned to its wartime configuration. Over the next few years it competed in multiple races and air displays, piloted by Wheeler and ex-ATA pilot Becky Sharpe until it was damaged as the result of a particularly heavy landing during the King's Cup at Southend on June 20, 1953.

Due to the damage sustained in the landing, AB910 was purchased by Vickers Armstrong Ltd and frequently used by the Supermarine test pilot Jeffrey Quill, as a tribute to 92 Squadron

G-AISU 82, KING'S CUP AIR RACE, 1949

and a variation of his initials QJ-J was worn over standard wartime camouflage. The code was applied in standard RAF letters but it did wear two schemes and for a while it had the serial applied under the wings. During this time the racing canopy was replaced with a non-armoured version.

Having been used as a hack for several years it was donated to the fledgling BBMF on September 15, 1965. Initially the previous scheme was retained but AB910 was pressed into service for the filming of the Battle of Britain and wore multiple codes and serials: AI-C, AI-D, AI-F, AI-J, AI-H, AI-M, AI-N, CD-D, CD-F, CD-K, DO-M, N3312, N3313, N3315, N3318, N3319 and N3321.

With the conclusion of filming the Spitfire was returned to the BBMF and it was decided to repaint AB910 to represent 145 Squadron's SO-T, but there was a mix-up and it returned from the paintshop with the code PB-T, which was soon corrected. 145 Sqn only wore the SO code from October 1939 until February 1942. During the Battle of Britain it used the Hurricane, only getting the Spitfire Mk.II in February 1942 and upgrading to the Mk.V in April, it will have been one of these aircraft that AB910 depicted.

AB910 returned to the markings of QJ-J yet again in 1972 when much thicker letters were applied with rounded corners and a sky band on the rear fuselage. This remained until 1976

G-AISU 40 KING'S CUP AIR RACE, 1951

when a new camouflage pattern was applied along with new code letters that had even more pronounced corners. While wearing this scheme AB910 had two incidents, the first relatively minor when an undercarriage leg collapsed at Duxford but the damage was relatively easy to repair.

The second incident put AB910 out of action for quite some time and was a serious accident. Over the weekend of August 19-20, 1978 an airshow was being held at Bex, Switzerland, with many aircraft, including AB910, remaining at the airfield over the weekend, before departing on the Monday. Flt Lt Pete Thorn sought and was given clearance to taxi to the end of the runway ready for take-off. At the same time, Harvard AT-16 PH-KMA was preparing to depart and was forced on to the runway to manoeuvre around a T-6 and Harrier that were also parked on the taxi way. Thorn began his take-off run and collided with the AT-16. The AT-16 pilot broke a leg but Thorn was unhurt.

AB910 required a major rebuild, which was undertaken at Abingdon. By 1981 it was airworthy again and fitted with a Merlin 35 engine, which had been taken from a Boulton Paul Balliol. This time it was given the markings of 603 City of Edinburgh Squadron's XT-M X4277. Flt Lt Richard Hillary took charge of the plane when it was delivered on August 28, 1940, and was flying it when he claimed his fifth kill, a Bf 109 on September 3. As the squadron engaged with more than 50

AB910 WITH NO MARKINGS FOLLOWING REPAIRS, 1956

German fighters Hillary saw hits upon the wings and engine but continued to press home the attack and was hit himself. The cockpit caught fire and the hood was stuck at first. Having released his straps and freeing the hood Hillary turned X4277 on its back and passed out. He came round in the air, deployed his parachute and then found himself in the North Sea. Hillary was badly burned and treated by the plastic surgeon and founder of the Guinea Pig Club, Archibald McIndoe, who rebuilt his face, creating new eyelids and lips along with re-growing the lost flesh on his hands. Despite the restriction of movement in his hands, Hillary eventually returned to flying duties and was sent to 54 OTU for bomber conversion. During one training exercise on January 8, 1943, he and his crewmate Sgt Wilfred Fison were undertaking a night training flight in Scotland during poor weather when they crashed in Berwickshire, Scotland.

The next change of markings for AB910 was in 1986 with BP-O of 457 Squadron RAAF 'In Memory of R J Mitchell'. The original Mk.Ia X4936 was one of two given by Frederick Pearson, an American multi-millionaire living at Sulbry Hall, Rugby. The full official inscription was 'From an American in Memory of R J Mitchell'. X4936 was delivered to 6 MU at Brize Norton on February 1, 1941, remaining there until the newly-formed 457 Sqn RAAF took charge of it on June 23 at Baginton, using the Mk.Ia Spitfire while working up to operational readiness.

SUPERMARINE SPITFIRE MK.Vb AB910

QJ-J, VICKERS, FIRST OF FOUR VARIATIONS OF THE SCHEME WORN WITH TYPE C ROUNDELS, 1956

With newer marks of Spitfire becoming available, X4936 was relegated to training duties when it was transferred to 58 OTU at Grangemouth on October 22. In March 1942 it suffered damage and was sent away for repairs before being returned to the unit. It lasted until November 10 when it was damaged again with Sgt Pritchard at the controls during a heavy landing. Following the repairs, completed in June 1943, it was sent to 45 MU at Kinloss until allocated to 17 Service Flying Training School at Cranwell on July 12. X4936 was damaged again on August 19 when Lt C Vazicio, practicing air-to-air combat in it, collided with Lt S Ural's Spitfire P7374. Fortunately, both pilots were unharmed and made safe landings. X4936 was repaired for a final time and sent to Yeovilton, joining 748 NAS on January 15, 1944.

This time it remained in one piece for several weeks before being severely damaged on March 31 when Sub-Lt Foxley over ran the perimeter fence. Although it was possible to repair X4936, this time it was not repaired.

P/O George Herman Bennions' Spitfire Mk.Ia X4559 EB-J of 41 Sqn was the subject of the next scheme in 1990. This Mk.Vb also wore the text 'The Guinea Pig Club' on the fuselage as Bennions was a founder member due to the burns he suffered when he was shot down in X4559. Bennions had first joined 41 Sqn in January 1936 while it was flying the Hawker Demon in Aden and remained with the squadron until the Battle of Britain.

QJ-J VICKERS, SECOND ITERATION WITH TYPE A.1 ROUNDEL, 1960

Having already claimed 12 destroyed, five probable and five damaged, he was called into action on October 1 shortly before he was due to go on leave and having just received news that he had been awarded a DFC.

The squadron engaged a force of Bf 109s near Brighton and he bagged one before receiving a direct cannon shell hit to the cockpit. The explosion caused damage to his right arm and leg as well as blinding him. Bennions also suffered burns as he struggled to bail out. Once the parachute had been deployed he passed out. He was given emergency treatment at Horsham Hospital where they managed to save his right eye, the left being lost before being treated over the coming months for his burns by McIndoe and becoming a founder member of the Guinea Pig Club.

Bennions eventually recovered and returned to flying, although now only as a non-combatant during daylight hours and with a passenger. A posting to North Africa followed as liaison officer to an American Fighter Group in which he had the opportunity to fly Spitfires. He remained with them in Italy until he was injured in a landing craft in October 1943. Following the war, Bennions was discharged and became a teacher.

Between 1991 and 1993, AB910 once again wore the markings of 133 Eagle Sqn MD-E, previously worn in June/July 1942. This was followed by another wartime scheme, AE-H of 402 Sqn RCAF between 1994 and 1996. Over the winter, AB910 had its cannon fitted for the first time since 1949 and a temporary

SUPERMARINE SPITFIRE MK.Vb AB910

CD-D N331, TEMPORARY BATTLE OF BRITAIN FILM SCHEME, 1968

scheme was applied in early 1997 when it was given the code XR-A of 71 Eagle Squadron in preparation for an appearance at an airshow at Nellis AFB. It was dismantled and flown across the Atlantic in an RAF Hercules on April 4, 1997. Upon its return to Coningsby it was repainted as W3430 ZD-C of 222 Natal Sqn with the Warner Bros logo and 'President Roosevelt' just below the cockpit.

Warner Bros generously donated £45,000 to purchase three Mk.Vbs in 1941 with W3430 named after the president. It was taken on charge by the RAF on June 26, 1941, by 38 MU at Llandow with 72 Sqn receiving it on July 7 and using it for sweeps over the channel. W3430 joined 222 Sqn at North Weald on May 14, 1942, where it received the code ZD-C and remained with the squadron until November when it was put into storage. It remained there until it was shipped to Portugal in October 1943 and flown by the Portuguese Air Force until it retired the type in mid-1953 whereupon most, including W3430, were scrapped.

AB910 received desert camouflage with the next change of scheme in 2003 when Spitfire Mk.Vb AB502 IR-G of 244 Wing was the inspiration. AB502 was the personal plane for Wg Cdr Ian Richard 'Widge' Gleed while commanding 244 Wing in the Middle East. Gleed joined the RAF in 1936 and having completed his training on Christmas Day 1936 he was posted to 46 Sqn, which was then equipped with the Gloster Gauntlet II at Digby.

With the outbreak of war, Gleed was promoted to flight

AI-M N3321 TEMPORARY BATTLE OF BRITAIN FILM SCHEME, 1968

commander and posted to 266 Squadron, at that time flying the Fairey Battle but converting to the Spitfire Mk.I in January 1940. While testing N3120 on February 18 he found it breaking up around him and bailed out. Despite this, Gleed still required a three-week convalescence period for his injuries. In May he joined 87 Sqn, flying Hurricanes in France as A Flight commander. The two days after his arrival he became an ace, on May 18 two Bf 110s were claimed and the next day a Bf 109 E and two Do 17 Zs were destroyed, along with a shared He 111 and a probable Bf 109 E. The squadron returned to the UK and Gleed's tally continued to climb during the Battle of Britain. At the end of the year he was promoted to Squadron Leader and took command of 87 Sqn, with which he remained for the majority of 1941 flying Hurricanes.

Gleed became commander of Ibsley Wing, made up of 118, 234 and 501 squadrons, in November 1941 and for the first time his personal initials IR-G were applied to his Spitfire, as was the Wing Commander's prerogative and he was involved in bomber escorts and sweeps over the channel. This came to an end when he was rested from operations in July 1942. Unhappy with remaining behind a desk, Gleed volunteered for a posting to the Middle East where, on January 31, 1943, he took command of 244 Wing consisting of 73, 92, 145 squadrons as well as 1 Sqn SAAF and was later joined by the Polish Fighting Team, which

SUPERMARINE SPITFIRE MK.Vb AB910

PB-T, THE CODES APPLIED INCORRECTLY, 1969

was affiliated with 145 Sqn.

Although Gleed could have had a Spitfire Mk.IX, he preferred to fly the Mk.Vb, choosing AB502, which was painted in desert camouflage and had his initials in blue with a white outline. Also retaining the tradition of all Gleed's other aircraft he had the cartoon cat Figaro from the film Pinocchio applied to the starboard side, it being first used on Hurricane P2798, which he received when he joined 87 Sqn in France. All the panels with Figaro on were kept and are currently in storage, held by the RAF Museum.

While in Tunisia, Gleed continued to lead the wing from the front, claiming a Bf 109 on March 17, 1943. It was to be his last.

On April 16, while conducting a sweep over the Cap Bon area, the Spitfires engaged SM.82 transport aircraft and their Bf 109 fighter escort. During the ensuing melee both Gleed and his wingman were shot down, probably by the Luftwaffe ace Ernst-Wilhelm Reinert.

AB910 was next repainted in 2007 following a scheduled winter service in the markings of Polish ace Jan Zumbach's Spitfire EN951 RF-D of 303 Sqn while he was in command of the squadron. Zumbach joined the Polish Army in 1935 transferring to pilot training in 1936 and graduating in 1938 whereupon he was posted to 111 Eskadra MyŚliwska which was equipped with the PZL P.11 fighter. Following a week-long training exercise

SO-T 154 SQUADRON, 1969

Zumbach crashed his P.11 while returning to Warsaw on May 21, 1939. It took several months for him to recover from the injuries including a broken leg, by which time war had broken out.

Zumbach made his way via Romania to France so he could be involved in the war, flying the Arsenal VG-33, Morane 406 and Curtiss Hawk 75 against the Luftwaffe. Despite being shot down on one occasion he was uninjured and with the fall of France he made his way to England by ship due to a French commander confiscating his plane.

Arriving in Plymouth on June 19, 1940, Zumbach was instrumental in the formation of 303 Sqn at Northolt that September. Both he and the rest of the squadron were involved in some of the most intense fighting during the Battle of Britain, Zumbach getting eight with another probable during the battle. He stayed with 303 Sqn throughout 1941 and on October 13 he claimed one of the first Fw 190s downed by an Allied pilot, although he received damage during the exchange.

December 1941 saw Zumbach rested and posted to 58 OTU as an instructor, although he did manage to find time to fly the occasional unofficial patrol. This period lasted until he returned to 303 Sqn on March 20, 1942. Two months later Zumbach took command when he was promoted to squadron leader. Zumbach flew three Spitfire Vbs during his two stints with 303 Sqn, BM144, EP594 and lastly EN951. They all wore the code RF-D and had Donald Duck on the forward fuselage along with his kill tally.

He eventually left the squadron after another successful period

SUPERMARINE SPITFIRE MK.Vb AB910

QJ-J 92 SQUADRON WITH SKY BAND, 1971

on December 1, 1942, returning to operations as commander of 2nd Polish Air Wing, 133 Wing in February 1943, a post which lasted until January 1945 when Zumbach was transferred to HQ 84 Group. He ended the war as a POW having made a navigational error while flying an Auster on April 7 and finding himself out of fuel behind enemy lines. By the end of the war he had 12 confirmed, five probables, one damaged and two shared. After the war he flew contraband, smuggled diamonds, fought for the Katanga Air Force and led Biafran forces against Nigeria. Zumbach was a colourful character who died in mysterious circumstances in France on January 3, 1986.

For the 2013 and 2014 seasons, AB910 wore the 133 Sqn code MD-E for a third time. During the winter service the armoured windscreen was fitted and for the 2015 season it was painted in the markings of Spitfire Vb BM327 SH-F of 64 Sqn flown by Flt Lt Tony Cooper on D-Day. The RAF took charge of BM327 when it was delivered to 45 MU on March 29, 1942, and it served with 72, 92 and 66 squadrons between then and March 1944 when it was damaged and sent away for repairs. Airworthy again, BM327 arrived at 64 Sqn on May 22, 1944, just in time to be flown by Cooper during Operation Overlord. It was retired to 61 OTU on December 5 and struck by another Spitfire during take-off on December 16.

Cooper joined the RAF Volunteer Reserve in late 1937 having been previously rejected by the RAF due to a damaged ear drum. After ab initio training, where he was assessed as above

QJ-J 92 SQUADRON, 1976

average, he became a flying instructor first in England and later in Canada, arriving there in November 1940. Cooper repeatedly requested to be posted to an operational squadron and his wish was granted when he joined 64 Sqn based at Ayr during July 1943 and stayed with it until November 1944 when he was posted back to instructional flying.

On June 6, 1944, he flew two sorties, the first as cover for Utah beach with a pre-dawn take-off at 04.30 hours and later in the day over Omaha beach. The squadron including Cooper later flew in support of Operation Market Garden and before he left the unit he had become a flight commander.

By the time he retired from the RAF at the end of the war Cooper had survived five forced landings, one due to enemy fire, amassed 3,200 hours and flown 160 operational sorties. Cooper got to see AB910 painted up as his Spitfire before he passed away in 2016, days before his 101st birthday.

In 2023 it was decided that following the next service AB910 would once again wear the wartime scheme of 402 Sqn RCAF, extensive research was conducted to ensure greater accuracy than the last time the scheme was applied in 1994 when there were minor differences. The only major notable change with the latest iteration is the full serial being visible when, during the war it would have been obscured by the invasion stripes.

SUPERMARINE SPITFIRE MK.Vb AB910

XT-M 603 CITY OF EDINBURGH SQUADRON, REPRESENTING X4277, 1981

BP-O 'IN MEMORY OF R J MITCHELL' 457 SQUADRON ROYAL AUSTRALIAN AIR FORCE, REPRESENTING X4936, 1986

BATTLE OF BRITAIN MEMORIAL FLIGHT IN PROFILE

EB-J 41 SQUADRON, REPRESENTING X4559, 1990

XR-A 71 EAGLE SQUADRON, REPRESENTING BM510, APRIL 1997

SUPERMARINE SPITFIRE MK.Vb AB910

ZD-C 222 NATAL SQUADRON, REPRESENTING W3430, 1997

IR-G 244 WING, REPRESENTING AB502, 2003

BATTLE OF BRITAIN MEMORIAL FLIGHT IN PROFILE

RF-D 303 POLISH SQUADRON, REPRESENTING EN951, 2007

SH-F 64 SQUADRON, REPRESENTING BM327, 2015

SUPERMARINE SPITFIRE MK.Vb AB910

AB910 originally wore the scheme MD-E in June/July 1942, again from 1991-93 and again when photographed here in 2012. JOHNNY B

Early post war photo in bare metal having been purchased by Gp Capt Alan Wheeler for racing, 1949. E.J. RIDING, PETER ARNOLD COLLECTION

Converted to racing configuration and painted for the King's Cup Air Races, here at Hendon July 21, 1951. PETER ARNOLD COLLECTION

QJ-J still under ownership of Vickers with red spinner. SAN DIEGO AIR & SPACE MUSEUM

AE-H 402 SQUADRON, THIRD ITERATION OF THE SCHEME FIRST WORN IN JULY 1944, 2024

SUPERMARINE SPITFIRE MK.Vb AB910

BATTLE OF BRITAIN MEMORIAL FLIGHT IN PROFILE

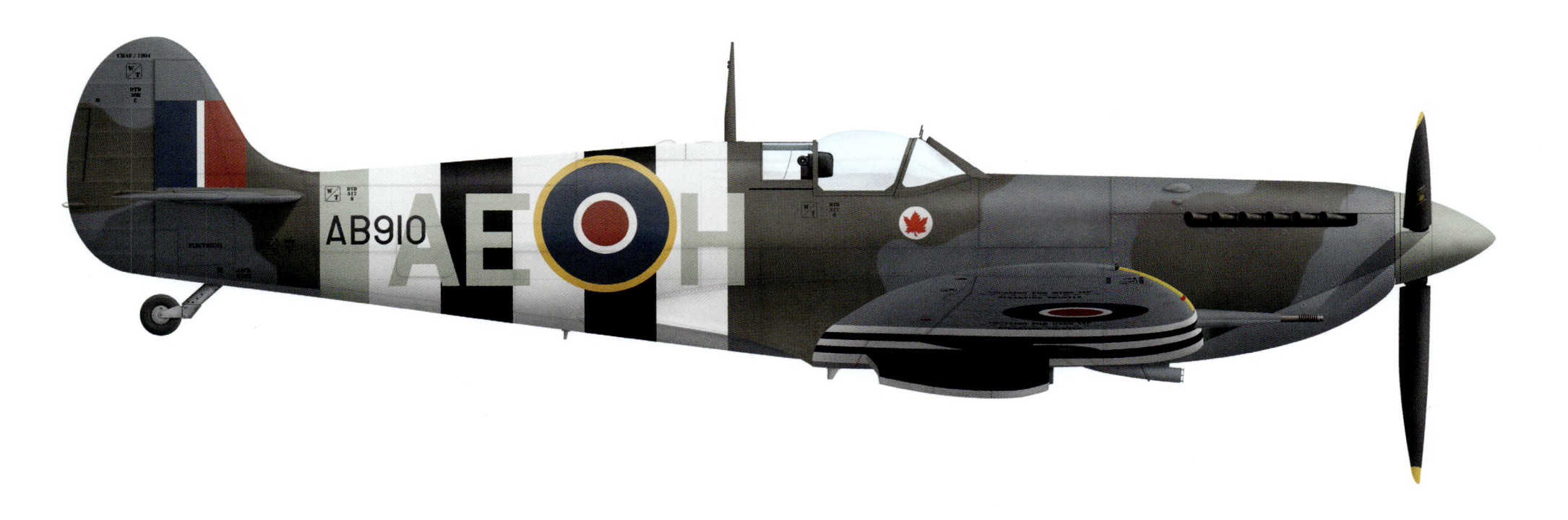

SUPERMARINE SPITFIRE MK.Vb AB910

Pictured in the early 1960s as QJ-J under the ownership of Vickers. L. Holden, Peter Arnold Collection

SUPERMARINE SPITFIRE MK.Vb AB910

One of several schemes worn during filming of Battle of Britain, 1968. TONY CLARKE

AB910 wore the code QJ-J in a variety of styles including a thicker version during the 1970s. DAVID WELCH

On August 21 1978 at Bex, Switzerland AB910 was involved in a ground collision with a Harvard. PETER RUSHEN

AB910 and the Harvard. PETER RUSHEN

SUPERMARINE SPITFIRE MK.Vb AB910

Following a major rebuild AB910 took to the air as XT-M, shown here at Swinderby in June 1983 with LF363 in the background. DAVID WELCH

Douglas Bader with Adolf Galland in the cockpit of Spitfire AB910. PETER RUSHIN

Bob Stanford Tuck, Douglas Bader, Geoffrey Page and Adolf Galland with BBMF crew. EDGARDO NESSI

AB910 XT-M outside the hangar at Coningsby. IAN POWELL

AB910 being prepared for a repaint circa 1992. ROB EVANS

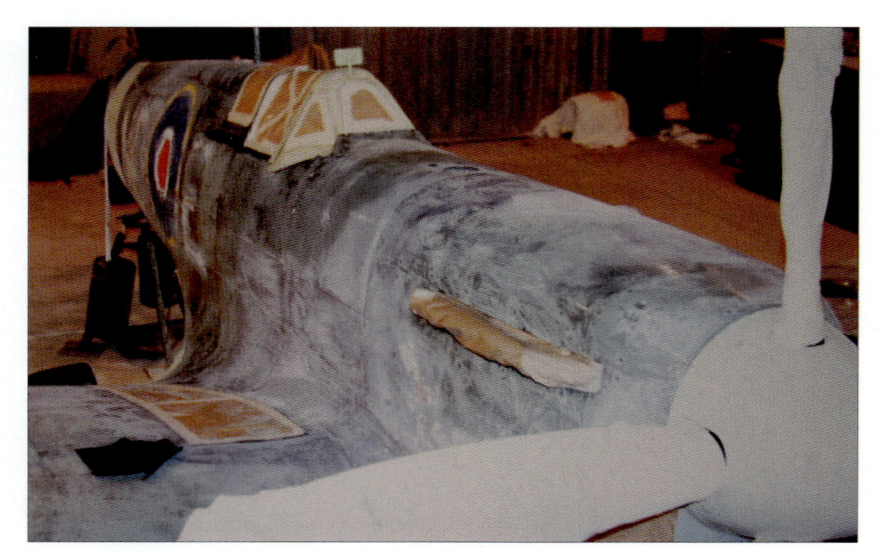

Sanded and masked ready for the new scheme. ROB EVANS

The camouflage pattern outline is applied freehand. ROB EVANS

AB910 in desert camouflage, 2004. Crown Copyright

Undergoing engine maintenance at Coningsby, showing Gleed's cartoon cat Figaro. JAMES KIGHTLY

Aerial shot of Zumbach's RF-D, May 2007. CROWN COPYRIGHT

AB910 in the hangar at Coningsby, 2011. AUTHOR

Detailed shot of RF-D nose art and kill markings. AUTHOR

In the hangar at Coningsby. AUTHOR

Waiting to take off with Typhoon ZK349 GN-A at Coningsby, April 2015.
Crown Copyright

The boss, Mark 'Disco' Discombe starting up AB910 at RAF Benson.
Lisa Harding

The cowling removed for routine work. AUTHOR

SUPERMARINE SPITFIRE LF.IXe MK356

Spitfire LF.IXe MK356 was flown with 443 (Hornet) Squadron RCAF in support of the Allied invasion of Normandy in 1944 and since then it has made three wheels-up landings while in service.

Somewhat unsurprisingly, MK356 was built at the Castle Bromwich factory and handed over to 9 Maintenance Unit at Cosford on February 4, 1944. On March 11 it was delivered to 443 Sqn, 114 Wing, at RAF Digby, where it was allocated to B Flight and given the squadron code 2I-V once a Merlin 66 engine had been fitted, presumably replacing the Merlin 63 it would have been built with. The new engine was optimised for low level flight, ideally below 25,000ft, hence the LF (Low Fighter) prefix to the designation.

A week later the squadron moved to Holmsley South, Hampshire, and began working up to operations. During the following weeks and months the squadron operated from several airfields along the south coast, including Westhampnett and Ford conducting escort and ground-attack missions on targets in France using a mix of bombs and strafing in preparation for D-Day.

The first of 60 wartime operations for MK356 took place on April 14 when the squadron flew a low level fighter sweep, known as a Rodeo, around Paris. It had to make wheels-up landings twice due to damage sustained but this was quickly repaired and MK356 returned to operational duties.

Like most aircraft within a squadron, MK356 was flown by a multitude of pilots but predominantly by the Canadian Flg Off Gordon Ockenden for 19 missions including two on June 6. The squadron flew a total of four patrols that day and although MK356 remained grounded for the first, it participated in the rest of them. Ockenden was in MK356 for missions taking off at 11.25am and 3.40pm, both lasting around two hours. For the

HAWKINGE GATE GUARDIAN, 1950

next patrol at 7.45pm Flg Off Arthur 'Art' Horrell was flying MK356. All three trips were recorded as uneventful, probably due to the air superiority the Allies had over Normandy during the invasion.

The next day during a patrol over the beaches, B flight encountered four Bf 109s near Caen. Both Ockenden and Flt Lt Hugh Russel engaged one of the aircraft and during the chase out to sea they scored multiple hits on it. Their combined firepower brought it down and, with no pilot clearly responsible, they claimed a half kill each, the only aerial victory for MK356.

Seven days later MK356 conducted its last flight for over half a century, signalling an end to only nine weeks of operational flying. While Flg Off Gordon Munro was taking off for a patrol over the beachhead from Ford one of the wheels fell off. But since the lack of a wheel did not impede the Spitfire's performance, he carried on with the mission and made the third belly-landing of MK356's career at 10.25am. Two days later, on June 16, the squadron moved to one of the advanced landing grounds in France, leaving MK356 behind.

83 Group Support Unit, based at Redhill, took custody of MK356 and it was placed into storage until after the war. Given the serial 5690M, it was transferred to Halton in October 1945 and used as an instructional airframe. In 1951 it was relegated to gate guardian duties, first placed on display at Hawkinge, where it was painted in all over silver and erroneously given the serial M5690. It was then repainted in an inaccurate scheme for the

HAWKINGE GATE GUARDIAN WITH MAINTENANCE SERIAL M5690 (5690M), 1954

second time when it was given the code 2J and painted in Dark Earth, Dark Green with Duck Egg Blue undersides.

MK356 moved to Bicester in 1961 before being placed on a pole at Locking in 1962. The Spitfire was then put in another early war scheme when it was pressed into service for the Battle of Britain film as a static Spitfire. With filming complete, MK356 was once more placed into storage at Henlow before becoming a part of the RAF Museum Reserve collection and transported to St Athan for display in the museum.

The BBMF looked into the feasibility of restoring a Mk.IX to flight in the late 1980s, with MK356 deemed to be in the best condition despite the wings and spar having been damaged at some stage in the past. The restoration took place at St Athan, led by Chief Technician Chris Bunn, with work commencing on the six-year project in January 1992.

The biggest change MK356 underwent was the fitting of a new pair of clipped wings taken from Spitfire Mk.XVI SL674. On November 7, 1997, BBMF CO Sqn Ldr Paul Day took MK356 for a test flight, its first time off the ground in over 53 years. Following further tweaks, MK356 arrived at Coningsby on November 14. Quite fittingly, the post-restoration scheme was the same one it had worn during the war, 2I-V of 443 Sqn RCAF.

MK356 was not to remain in the same scheme forever though, and following a winter service during which extended tips were fitted by the Aircraft Restoration Company at Duxford, MK356 appeared in an all over silver scheme for the 2008 season. Based on 601 (County of London) Squadron's MJ205 UF-Q, the scheme is thought to not be 100% accurate as photographs indicate it flew in bare metal but, for

MK355 HAWKINGE GATE GUARDIAN, 1960

ease of maintenance and corrosion control, the decision was taken to paint MK356. MJ250 was built at Castle Bromwich, handed over to the RAF on October 22, 1943, and joined 601 Sqn at Canne, Italy in December. The squadron flew in close ground support of the 8th Army as they advanced north through Italy with the majority of the missions either bombing or strafing targets.

Having been flown by various pilots in June 1944, MJ250 became the personal aircraft of Flt Lt Desmond Ibbotson, an ace with 11 victories who had returned to 601 Sqn for a second tour the previous November, originally having been with it in North Africa. Ibbotson continued to fly MJ250 until completing his second tour at the end of July, having flown 385 operational missions. He was then posted as an instructor to 5 Refresher Flying Unit at St Egidio and died during a Spitfire air test at the age of 23.

As an interesting aside, Ibbotson had been shot down in North Africa and taken prisoner where he was introduced to Rommel on November 7, 1942. The following night he escaped, made it through the front line and returned to flying. MJ250 was struck off charge on June 5, 1945, and scrapped.

Invasion stripes returned in 2014 when Spitfire Mk.IX ML214, 5J-K 'Kay' of 126 (Persian Gulf) squadron was applied. ML214 was flown by Ioannis Agorastos 'Johnny' Plagis DSO, DFC & Bar

SUPERMARINE SPITFIRE LF.IXe MK356

2J LOCKING GATE GUARDIAN, 1962

when he was the commanding officer of 126 Sqn. Plagis was the son of Greek immigrants to Rhodesia who went on to become an ace with 19 victories. He signed up when war broke out and, despite initially being turned down by the RAF, he was accepted the following year as Greece was involved in the war as an ally.

Once qualified he volunteered to serve in Malta with 249 Sqn, arriving in March 1942 and flying the Spitfire Mk.V. Remaining on the island he was transferred to 185 Sqn. With his tour complete in July he returned to the UK and became an instructor for the next year, but this rest period ended a year later when he was posted to 64 Squadron as the commanding officer in September 1943, based at Coltishall and flying the Mk.Vc over northern France.

Plagis' next move in July 1944 was to 126 Sqn which had recently returned from Malta. This coincided with his promotion to squadron leader and he chose ML214 as his personal plane. He picked K because his sister's name was Kay, and as with all the other aircraft Plagis flew he had her name applied by the cockpit. His victories were also added. With D-Day having only been a month before, the squadron aircraft retained the invasion stripes on the lower surfaces.

Plagis regularly flew ML214 over the continent — carrying out a range of missions from fighter escort to low level bombing. On one occasion, taking off for Osnabruck, Germany, to escort 100 Halifax bombers, ML214 lost its tail wheel. Plagis carried on and led the squadron, landing safely with no further damage to the aircraft nearly

BO-H N3317, TEMPORARY BATTLE OF BRITAIN FILM SCHEME, 1968

three hours later. His last flight in ML214 was on October 7, 1944, after which he flew NH395 5J-E, which not only had the name Kay, but also Muscat in English and Arabic having been presented by the Persian Gulf Fund. The squadron later converted to the Mustang III in December. Following the war Plagis flew Meteors as commander of first 234 and later 266 squadrons. Sadly, due to post-traumatic stress, Plagis committed suicide in 1974.

Neville Duke's Spitfire Mk.IXc EN152 QJ-3 of 92 Squadron in desert camouflage was picked for the next scheme following the winter 2016/2017 service. Duke not only had an impressive wartime record but as a post-war test pilot he became a household name and held the world airspeed record in 1953. During the war Duke first served with 92 Sqn at Biggin Hill flying the Spitfire Mk.V before being posted to North Africa where he flew the P-40 Tomahawk with 112 Sqn. 92 Sqn had been posted to the region and, in November 1942, Duke returned to the squadron, which was flying the tropical variant of the Spitfire Mk.V.

The Mk.V Trop had inferior performance to the Bf 109 F and G as well as the Fw 190 being used by the Luftwaffe. To meet them on equal terms, 92 Sqn became the first in North Africa to

MK356 WITH SKY BAND, 1969

receive the Mk.IX with Duke leading a flight that picked up the first 12 from Algiers on March 23, 1943. One of the planes collected was EN152, QJ-3 which was used as the inspiration for MK356's scheme. Due to the Mk.V still being operated the new Spitfires were allocated an aircraft number instead of letter to help easily identify the different marks and pilots regularly flew whichever Spitfire was available for them instead of having personal aircraft.

EN152 was built at Chattis Hill, Hampshire, delivered to 9 MU on December 20, 1942, and shipped to Gibraltar the following month where it was then ferried to Algiers for collection. Duke departed 92 Sqn following his promotion to squadron leader for 73 OTC as chief flying instructor in June 1944, he was later given command of 145 Sqn in Italy. The following month the squadron replaced their Mk.IXs including EN152 with Mk.VIIIs; EN152 was transferred to 94 Sqn and coded GO-S. It was struck off charge on March 14, 1946.

MK356 was painted in the desert scheme to pay tribute to all those who fought in North Africa as part of the Desert Air Force, although it is not the first time the BBMF has flown a Spitfire in such a scheme, AB910 having worn similar camouflage between 2003 and 2006. It also recognises the amazing record of Neville Duke, the highest-scoring Allied ace in the Mediterranean theatre and post-war record-breaking test pilot.

BATTLE OF BRITAIN MEMORIAL FLIGHT IN PROFILE

2I-V 433 SQUADRON RCAF, RAF MUSEUM RESERVE COLLECTION REPRESENTING TD341, 1971

2I-V 433 SQUADRON RCAF WITH INVASION STRIPES, 1982

SUPERMARINE SPITFIRE LF.IXe MK356

2I-V 433 SQUADRON RCAF WITH REVISED CODES, 1997

UF-Q 601 COUNTY OF LONDON SQUADRON, REPRESENTING MJ250, 2008

BATTLE OF BRITAIN MEMORIAL FLIGHT IN PROFILE

5J-K 126 SQUADRON, REPRESENTING ML214, 2014

A lineup of Spitfires with MK356 in the foreground, AB910 in the middle, P7350 next to it and Chipmunk WK518 at the far end. AUTHOR

QJ-3 92 SQUADRON, REPRESENTING EN333, 2017

SUPERMARINE SPITFIRE LF.IXe MK356

BATTLE OF BRITAIN MEMORIAL FLIGHT IN PROFILE

SUPERMARINE SPITFIRE LF.IXe MK356

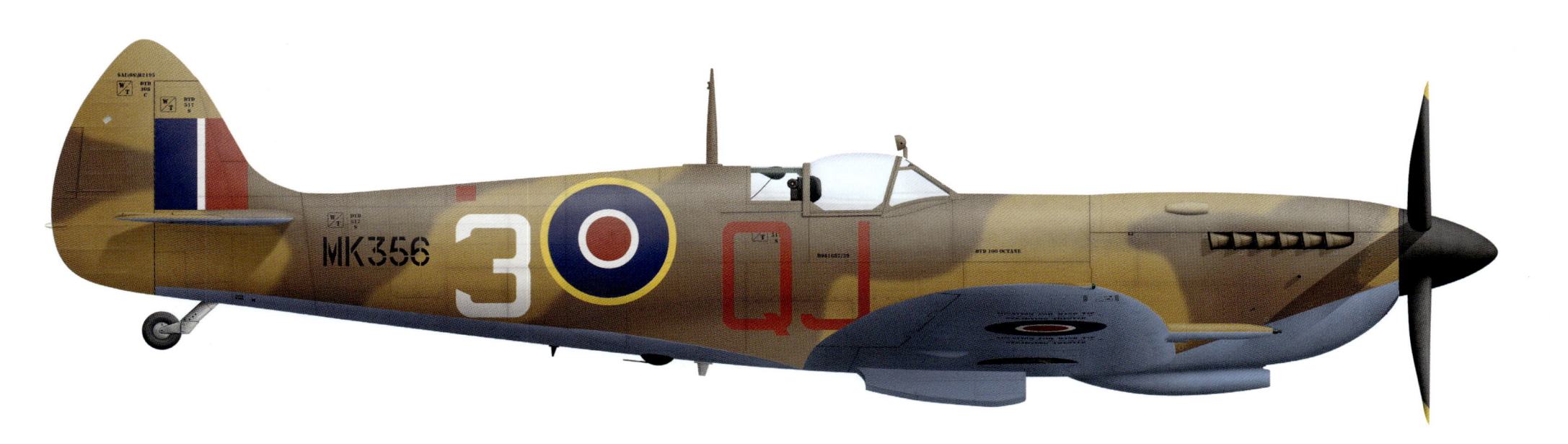

BATTLE OF BRITAIN MEMORIAL FLIGHT IN PROFILE

MK356 at Hawkinge wearing maintenance serial with WAAFs working out, November 17, 1954. PETER ARNOLD COLLECTION

MK356 once again in camouflage as Hawkinge's gate guardian. PETER ARNOLD COLLECTION

During the early 70s MK356 joined the RAF Museum Reserve Collection at St Athan. PETER ARNOLD COLLECTION

SUPERMARINE SPITFIRE LF.IXe MK356

MK356 on display as 2I-V, 2003. James Kightly

At Locking MK356 was mounted on a pole and painted in an approximate scheme using locally mixed paints, circa 1964. Peter Arnold Collection

An inverted MK356 UF-Q at Duxford September 2011 airshow. Tony Hisgett

BATTLE OF BRITAIN MEMORIAL FLIGHT IN PROFILE

'Kay' flying formation with Hurricane LF363 JX-B, September 2014.
ALAN WILSON

SUPERMARINE SPITFIRE LF.IXe MK356

MK356 tied down during winter service at Coningsby, December 2017. AUTHOR

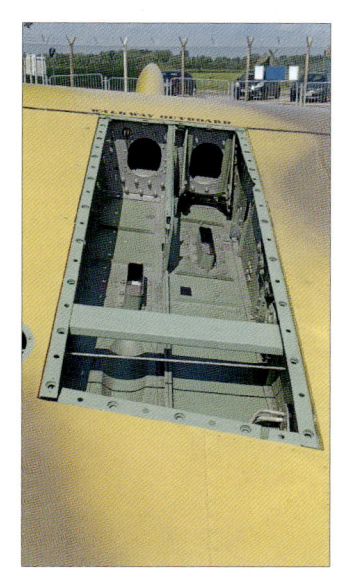

The port gun bays showing. AUTHOR

Detailed shot of 'Kay' and Plagis' kill markings. AUTHOR

5J-J flying into the evening sun, September 2014. ALAN WILSON

95

Sharing the runway with a Typhoon. LISA HARDING

SUPERMARINE SPITFIRE LF.IXe MK356

MK356 being prepared for an engine test. AUTHOR

TE311 flying into a Lincolnshire sunset LISA HARDING

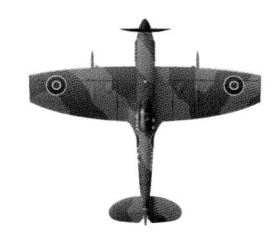

SUPERMARINE SPITFIRE Mk.XVIe TE311

Spitfire Mk.XVIe TE311 is the BBMF's most recent acquisition. For the first six years it was not officially intended to return to flying, but BBMF engineers worked on it during their spare hours until its return to flight was officially approved by the MoD.

TE311 was constructed at the Castle Bromwich factory and delivered on June 8, 1945. Too late to see action, it was placed in storage for a few months under the care of 39 Maintenance Unit, Colerne. On October 5, it was taken out of storage and allocated to the Empire Central Flying School's Handling Squadron based at Hullavington, remaining there until February 17, 1946, when it was returned to storage, this time into the care of 33 MU at Lyneham.

The Spitfire was pulled back out of storage five years later when it was allocated to 1689 Ferry Pilot Training Flight at Aston Down on May 31, 1951. The following month, on the 21st, a tyre burst during landing and TE311 was sent to Vickers Armstrong for repairs and eventually returned to flying duties on December 31. On July 31, 1952, it was transferred to the Ferry Training Unit at Benson and remained there until it was returned to 33 MU and back into temporary storage on September 23, 1953. January saw TE311 back in the air when it spent a month with No. 2 Civilian Anti-Aircraft Co-operation Unit at Langham but it was soon back in storage at Lyneham on February 23, 1954. On December 13, it was officially transferred to non-flying status.

In August 1955 it was painted all over silver, given the maintenance serial 7241M and put on display at Tangmere as the gate guardian. Here TE311 remained until called upon for the Battle of Britain film. It was loaned to Spitfire Productions Ltd in 1967 and heavily modified with the rear fuselage built up to make it look like a high-backed early variant, the pointed rudder was replaced with a rounded one and a bubble canopy temporarily fitted. It was also restored to a taxiing condition. With filming completed in 1968 the changes to TE311 were reversed and a Dark Green and Dark

TANGMERE GATE GUARDIAN, NO SERIAL, 1957

Earth scheme was applied with non-standard roundels and in this condition it was placed on display at Benson.

TE311 was not to remain at Benson for long before carrying on its nomadic journey. Having been on static display at the Battle of Britain Display on September 20, 1968, it was transferred to the RAF Exhibition Flight, based at Abingdon, where it toured the country in a variety of schemes over the next couple of decades. The last scheme it wore was a Dark Grey and Dark Sea Grey scheme with invasion stripes, the serial and code MK178 LZ-V. In this scheme it was placed on the flight line at one Duxford show but never flew.

TE311 was initially going to be put up for sale in 1999 but instead it was given to the BBMF along with Spitfire LF.XVI TB382 to be used as spares for the flying Spitfires in October 1999. Despite the poor condition TE311 was in, the decision was taken by engineers led by Chief Technician Paul Blackah to work on restoring it during their spare time in October 2001.

Initially, the intention was to replace damaged and corroded parts and work progressed at a slow pace until 2005 when they realised that instead of remaining a hangar queen there was a realistic possibility that it could be returned to flight.

In 2007, the Ministry of Defence officially sanctioned the restoration project to return TE311 to flight and the wings were overhauled by Airframe Assemblies Ltd. In lieu of payment they received what was left of TB382 which had already been broken up for spares. It took a further five years of work but, on October

SUPERMARINE SPITFIRE Mk.XVIe TE311

TANGMERE GATE GUARDIAN, 1960

19, 2012, Sqn Ldr Ian Smith took TE311 up for a test flight.

Even before TE311 was returned to flight, it was painted in a tribute scheme — that of Spitfire Mk.XVIe TB675 4D-V of 74 Squadron flown by Sqn Ldr Tony Reeves, the commanding officer of the squadron during the last few months of the war in Europe. Reeves first joined the squadron in April 1943 while it was based in the Middle East flying the Hurricane Mk.IIb which was soon exchanged for the Spitfire Mk.Vb.

A year later, both Reeves and the squadron returned to the UK for the build-up for Operation Overlord in April 1944 by which time they were flying the Spitfire Mk.IXe. Following the invasion, the squadron moved to France in the September, joining the 2nd Tactical Air Force based near Antwerp. The squadron undertook a range of missions from flying fighter escort with Typhoons and Mitchells to close support bombing ground targets near the front line.

In March 1945 a number of Mk.XVIs were delivered to fly with the Mk.IXe. Included within this batch was TB675, 4D-V which Reeves took for his personal aircraft, although it was used regularly by other pilots including the commander of 145 Wing, Wg Cdr 'Sammy' Sampson when his own Spitfire was unavailable. Just before VE Day TB675 was transferred to 485 Sqn while 74 Sqn returned to the UK to re-equip with the Meteor. The Spitfire went on to serve with 341 Sqn and 84 Group Disbandment Centre until struck off charge on December 11, 1953.

In late 2016, TE311 underwent a thorough service and in preparation for the new scheme it was stripped followed by the application of an all over matt black primer with the serial applied to the rear fuselage.

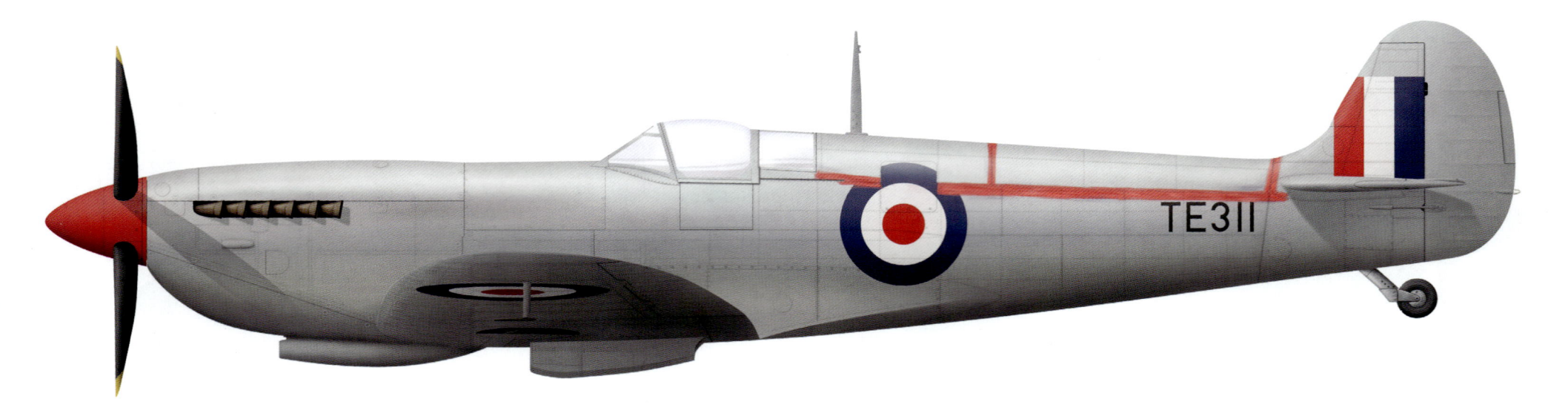

MARK ADDIE SPITFIRE HIGH BACK CONVERSION, BATTLE OF BRITAIN FILM, 1968

The rudder, elevators and undercarriage doors were all painted in anticipation of the new scheme. Due to the Typhoons taking precedence in the paint shop at Coningsby, the decision was taken to delay applying the full scheme until the end of the year. As Spitfire Mk.IX MK356 was unavailable due to a major service and Spitfire PR.XIX PM631 was lacking an engine, it was decided to fly TE311 in this unusual scheme for the 2017 display season in order to fulfil the BBMF's commitments for the year.

Although the new scheme was announced in November 2016, it was not until 2018 that TE311 finally flew in the markings of Spitfire Mk.XVI TD240 SZ-G, the personal aircraft of Gp Capt Aleksander Gabszewicz, 131 (Polish) Wing Commanding Officer. Having previously commanded 316 Sqn he decided to retain the squadron code (SZ) along with his initial when given the opportunity to pick his personalised code. Gabszewicz entered the military when he joined the Polish Army in 1932 but transferred to the air force, qualifying as a pilot in 1937. Two years later, during the German invasion, he shared credit for downing a He 111 in a PZL P.11. Following the fall of Poland, he made his way to France via Romania, Yugoslavia and Italy. He fought with the French Air Force and in a Bloch MB 152 he bagged a Do 17. With France overrun, Gabszewicz travelled to Britain via North Africa.

He fought with 607 Sqn in the last weeks of the Battle of Britain followed by a period with 303 Sqn and, in February 1941, he joined the newly-formed 316 Sqn with whom he retained a

AI-M N3321, TEMPORARY BATTLE OF BRITAIN FILM SCHEME, 1968

close affiliation. When the CO Sqn Ldr Wilczewski was shot down over France, Gabszewicz was given command of the squadron in November 1941. Having been rested from front line operations in the summer of 1942 he was promoted to Wing Commander in January 1943, taking over No 2 (Polish) Wing. In this role Gabszewicz brought his tally to nine-and-a-half destroyed, one-and-a-half probables and two damaged. A further promotion followed in February 1944 when Gabszewicz became a group captain and was responsible for 18 Sector within the 2nd Tactical Air Force. Then, in June 1944, he found himself commanding 131 Wing, leading them from airfields in France and later Germany. It was at Nordhorn, Germany, that the wing received its first Spitfire Mk.XVI — TD240 — which Gabszewicz claimed for himself. To distinguish the aircraft he had his choice of code letter applied along with the Group Captain pennant, the Polish roundel and, just like on previous Spitfires, a boxing dog, albeit somewhat larger this time.

With the war ended in Europe, Gabszewicz became a staff officer and TD240 passed to Sqn Ldr Boleslaw Kaczmarek of 302 Sqn who changed the code to WX-V and in October 1945 it was written off as the result of a belly landing caused by engine failure. Gabszewicz remained in the UK after the war, becoming Coltishall's station commander and later retiring to the Malverns.

The new scheme was selected for TE311 in early 2020 following the next planned service that commenced in the summer of 2021. Work on researching the scheme and preparing the artwork, including stencil details, can take several months to finalise and prepare. In part due to the ties the BBMF has with the Royal Netherlands Air Force Historic

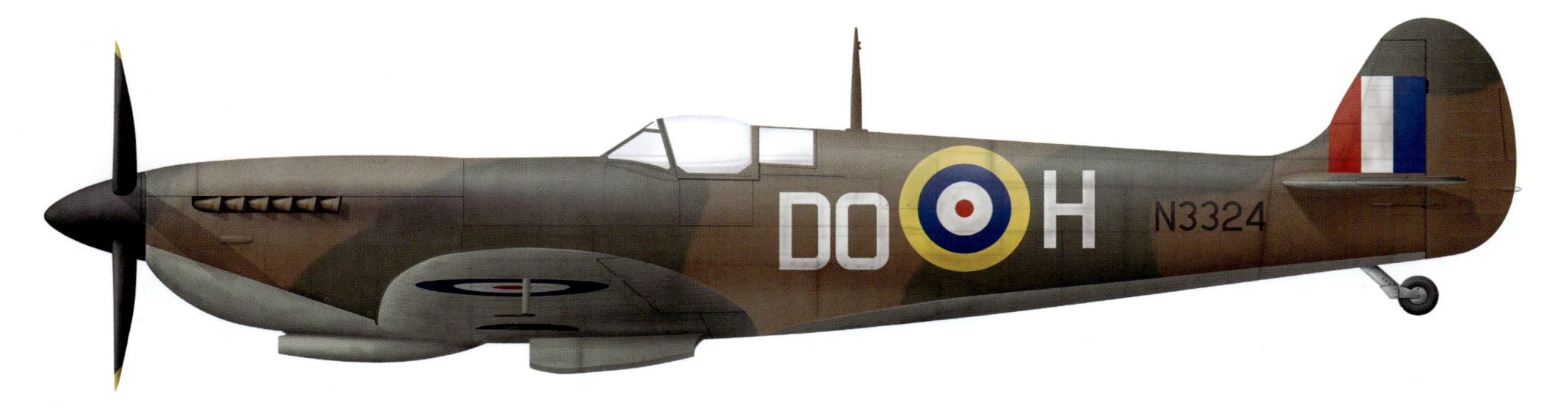

DO-H N3324, TEMPORARY BATTLE OF BRITAIN FILM SCHEME, 1968

Flight a scheme from the oldest Dutch squadron to serve with the RAF during WWII was chosen.

The squadron consisted of a core of Dutch personnel who had previously been attached to 167 Sqn along with eight Dutch pilots, the remaining 17 coming from the RAF. It was officially formed on June 12, 1943 at RAF Woodvale and from then until the following March it flew the Spitfire Mk.Vb & Mk.Vc. These were replaced by the Griffon engine Mk.XIV on June 20, 1944 during a squadron move south to RAF West Malling and remained there until that August, where the squadron was tasked with intercepting V1 flying bombs during 'Anti-Diver' patrols. The squadron then moved to the continent, relocating to Advanced Landing Ground B-79 Woensdrecht in the Netherlands, an airfield that had been established by the RNLAF in 1934 and subsequently occupied by the Luftwaffe—the squadron had come home. However, the move coincided with re-equipping the squadron with the Merlin-engined Spitfire Mk.IX. From there they flew missions that aided the allied ground forces, strafing and bombing targets while also flying in close air support for the advancing troops.

TD322 was chosen as the new scheme TE311 would represent, and just like TE311, TD322 was constructed as a clipped wing, low back Mk.XVIe at the Castle Bromwich factory. But unlike TE311 it made it into active service before the end of the war.

POST BATTLE OF BRITAIN CONVERSION TO ORIGINAL CONFIGURATION, 1968

322 Sqn was at ALG B.106 Twente, an airfield close to the Belgian border in the Netherlands when TD322 was delivered on April 20, 1945. Upon arrival it was in standard factory colours and the code 3W-M was applied. At some later stage the orange triangle used as the RNLAF roundel was applied, along with the squadron badge and mascot, Polly Grey, a red-tailed parrot. It is unclear exactly when the two markings were applied and it is conceivable that they appeared after VE Day, but this is the scheme that was selected.

During the final weeks of the war TD322 had the opportunity to attack multiple ground targets while flying armed reconnaissance missions. Following the war TD322 went on to serve with 349 Sqn, officially being transferred on October 18, 1945, but it was involved in an accident on March 21, 1946 and officially struck off charge four days later.

322 Sqn currently flies the F-35A and still has a red tailed parrot on the squadron as a tribute to the original Polly Grey who was brought into the squadron fold by Dutch P/O N W Sluyter in late July 1943. It is reported that the bird flew in a Spitfire (in a box) and also was encouraged to enjoy gin to the point of intoxication.

TE311 may have only had a short flying career so far with the BBMF in comparison to the other aircraft on the flight but through the passion of the engineers at Coningsby it fills a gap in the Spitfire lineage currently flown by the RAF.

BATTLE OF BRITAIN MEMORIAL FLIGHT IN PROFILE

BENSON GATE GUARDIAN, 1971

RAF EXHIBITION FLIGHT, 1973

SUPERMARINE SPITFIRE Mk.XVIe TE311

X4474 QV-I 19 SQUADRON, 1990

MK178 LZ-V 66 SQUADRON 1998

BATTLE OF BRITAIN MEMORIAL FLIGHT IN PROFILE

4D-V 74 SQUADRON, REPRESENTING TB675, 2012

TEMPORARY BLACK PRIMER SCHEME, 2017

SUPERMARINE SPITFIRE Mk.XVIe TE311

SZ-G 131 (POLISH) WING, REPRESENTING TD240, 2018

BATTLE OF BRITAIN MEMORIAL FLIGHT IN PROFILE

3W-M 322 (DUTCH) SQUADRON REPRESENTING TD322, 2023

SUPERMARINE SPITFIRE Mk.XVIe TE311

BATTLE OF BRITAIN MEMORIAL FLIGHT IN PROFILE

SUPERMARINE SPITFIRE Mk.XVIe TE311

Stripped to bare metal TE311 was exposed to the elements during the 50s and 60s as Tangmere gate guardian. DAVID WELCH

TE311 in the process of being temporarily converted to a high back Spitfire for the Battle of Britain film. PETER ARNOLD COLLECTION

Photograph of TE311 prior to full camouflage being added at Benson, 1969. DAVID WELCH

As part of the RAF Exhibition Flight TE311 toured the country, here it is on display in Wolverhampton in 1975. DAVID WELCH

SUPERMARINE SPITFIRE Mk.XVIe TE311

With filming completed TE311 reverted to the original configuration, work being carried out at Duxford, 1968.
PETER ARNOLD COLLECTION VIA SHUTTLEWORTH TRUST

The clipped wings of TE311 are clearly visible during this test flight at Coningsby, 2016.
Alan Wilson

SUPERMARINE SPITFIRE Mk.XVIe TE311

A static TE311 at Abingdon during the 70s in the RAF Exhibition Flight.
IAN POWELL

TE311 on final approach. TONY CLARKE

TE311 being stripped ready for a repaint in February 2017, the repaint was delayed by 12 months. TONY CLARKE

Continuing the stripping of TE311. BBMF

TE311 touching down at RIAT. Rob Monfea

SUPERMARINE SPITFIRE Mk.XVIe TE311

The difference in the angle of the undercarriage between the Mk.XVIe and the Mk.Vb AB910 in the background. AUTHOR

TE311 undergoing full winter service with PA474 in the background. AUTHOR

Due to display commitments TE311 performed in the matt black scheme for the 2017 display season. ALAN WILSON

TE311 wearing the markings of TD240, 131 (Polish) Wing. ROB MONFEA

Flames leaping out during an engine start. CROWN COPYRIGHT

PM631 in the hangar while with THUM. David Welch

SUPERMARINE SPITFIRE Mk.XIX PM631

Of all the historic warbirds operated by the BBMF, Spitfire Mk.XIX PM631 is the youngest but it remains a tribute to those airmen who flew unarmed over enemy territory.

Constructed at Reading after the war, PM631 was handed over to the RAF when it arrived at Brize Norton on November 6, 1945. It was immediately placed into storage with 6 Maintenance Unit where it remained. It was eventually taken out of storage and delivered to 203 Advanced Flying School, Driffield in May 1949 as a trainer for pilots.

The aircraft was taken off flying duties in January 1950, initially returning to 6 MU and later being transferred to 9 MU at Cosford. During early 1951 it spent a brief period at Buckenburg Air Base, Germany, before returning to 9 MU for conversion work to prepare it for meteorological duties in July 1951. The Temperature and Humidity Flight was not formed until April 1951 but was created to carry out meteorological flights for the Central Forecasting Office at Dunstable.

Until this point the work had been carried out by RAF units but the creation of a dedicated flight freed up resources elsewhere. Initially, the flight consisted of three Spitfire Mk.XIXs, PM549, PM577 and PM652, and these were later joined by three more — PS853, PS915 and of course PM631, all three going on to form the core of the Historic Aircraft Flight later in the decade. On July 13, 1951, the flight moved to Woodvale and remained there until it was eventually disbanded.

Continual high-altitude flying naturally took its toll on the airframes and they were replaced by Mosquitos with the final meteorological flight by a Spitfire taking place on June 10, 1957. Details of the decision to provide the three Mk.XIXs to the fledgling HAF, then at Biggin Hill, are covered elsewhere, but PM631 has remained with the HAF and latterly the BBMF ever since.

PM631 was involved in trials flying mock combat against Lightnings during dissimilar combat trials at the Central Fighter Establishment in 1963. In the early 1960s there was a distinct possibility of a conflict between British and Indonesian forces during the formation of Malaysia. The Indonesian Air Force

PM631 UU-T 226 OPERATIONAL CONVERSION UNIT, 1949

was flying antiquated P-51 Mustangs and tactics needed to be developed allowing the Sea Vixens of 893 NAS and Javelins of 60 Sqn to successfully engage them despite the speed discrepancies. PM631 did not complete the trials due to engine problems so Mk.XIX PS853 was flown instead by Wing Commander John Nicholls. This aircraft had been relegated to a gate guardian at Binbrook but, at the insistence of the station CO, it was maintained in flying condition.

It was found that the Spitfire had a tighter turning circle than the Lightning so it was futile to become involved in a turning dogfight. And due to the low heat signature from the Mustang's exhausts, gaining a missile lock was highly challenging. A straight pass and gun attack was also ruled out — the high closing speed reducing accuracy on a small target.

The method that was found to bring the greatest chance of shooting down a slow moving target was for the Lightning to dive down and then make a climbing attack to the rear. The climb rate was such that the Spitfire or Mustang could not hope to retaliate if the first attack failed. By the time Lightnings were deployed to Malaysia in 1966, however, the situation had de-escalated.

Inevitably, PM631 was called upon to appear in the Battle of Britain film during 1968 and had multiple serials and codes applied during the year over a temporary Dark Green and Dark Earth scheme. With filming complete, PM631 was returned to its standard PR configuration and painted in the markings of AD-C

TEMPERATURE AND HUMIDITY FLIGHT 1950

of 11 Squadron with a Dark Sea Grey and Dark Green camouflage. It was not until after the war that 11 Sqn was equipped with the Spitfire Mk.XIV and XVIII but, having been in the Far East since April 1942, it remained there in the post-war years until disbanded in February 1948. It did, however, re-form the following year in Germany with the Mosquito FB VI and later the Vampire, Javelin and Lightning. It currently operates the Typhoon.

The scheme was kept for 14 years until a repaint for the 1984 season when PM631 kept the grey/green camouflage but had invasion markings painted on the lower surfaces when it represented Spitfire Mk.XXI DL-E LA200 of the first front line unit in the RAF to convert to the Mk.XXI, with aircraft beginning to arrive over the winter of 1944/45. In April the squadron moved from Manston to Ludham, Norfolk and it began flying over Holland in sweeps.

Due to allied dominance in Western Europe, targets were scarce even when the squadron switched to searching for V2 launch sites and by the middle of the month it had commenced anti-submarine patrols off the Dutch coast. On May 12, F/O Geoffrey Kay was undertaking aerobatics near Ludham in LA200 when the Spitfire crashed, killing him.

PM631 was repainted in 1990 in South East Asia Command colours, depicting the low-backed Spitfire Mk.XIV MV363 N 'Mary' of 11 Squadron. MV363 first flew on February 2, 1945, but did not reach the squadron based at Chettinad, India, until the end of June having been

HISTORIC AIRCRAFT FLIGHT DELIVERY SCHEME, 1957

crated up and transported by sea.

Following the capitulation of Japan the squadron, including MV363, moved to Malaya and as part of the occupation forces it was stationed in Japan until it temporarily disbanded in February 1948. MV363 remained in Japan and was officially struck off charge the following month on March 24.

PM631's scheme changed again in 1996, back to PRU Blue in the livery of a Mk.XIX of 681, retaining the SEAC roundels but losing the white SEAC bands to represent one of the Spitfires used by 681 Squadron. The squadron was formed as a photo reconnaissance unit out of 3 PRU at Dum Dum, India on January 2, 1943, and carried out this role in the Far East until it disbanded. Initially, the squadron used a mix of Hurricane Mk.IIs and Spitfire Mk.IVs for the PR role.

During the year it also flew the Mosquito for a period but by the start of 1944 it was almost exclusively using PR variants of the Spitfire with the PR.XI arriving in October 1943, the Mosquitos being used as the core of the newly-formed 681 Squadron.

Shortly before the squadron left Mingaladon, Myanmar, the first Spitfire PR.XIXs began arriving in August 1945. During the post-war years the squadron moved to other RAF stations around the Far East, carrying on in the photo reconnaissance role. The squadron was eventually disbanded on August 1, 1946, at Palam, Punjab and renumbered as 34 Squadron.

HISTORIC AIRCRAFT FLIGHT FIRST CAMOUFLAGE SCHEME, 1957

PM631 had invasion stripes applied in 2002 to represent an early Mk.XIX that would have been used by 541 Squadron for high altitude reconnaissance over Europe during the war. A typical flight over mainland Europe would have lasted around four hours and to accommodate this endurance the PR.XIXs were stripped of non-essential items such as cannon to keep their weight down and provide a range of 1500 miles.

Apart from the first 25 built, they all had pressurised cockpits with missions typically flown at around 30,000ft. Flt Lt Ray 'Arty' Holmes was with 514 Sqn when he was tasked with a trip to Hamburg to photograph the quays. Holmes was the fourth to attempt the flight, the three previous pilots having failed to return. Due to poor weather during take-off and landing he was reliant on the instruments. Over the Dutch coast German radar picked up and locked onto him, Holmes' radio picking up the distinctive wail. As he neared the target he was spotted by an Me 262 that had been scrambled to intercept the lone Spitfire, but there was time for a pass so the Spitfire levelled off and the two offset cameras (to produce stereoscopic images) began taking photographs every 2.5 seconds. Holmes having completed a first pass over the docks, the Me 262 dived to intercept but by reducing airspeed and entering a high-speed stall the Me 262 overshot.

Holmes knew it would take several minutes for the German to turn and find him again so he had time for a second pass before entering cloud as a second Me 262 closed in on him. Returning he found

HISTORIC AIRCRAFT FLIGHT FIRST CAMOUFLAGE SCHEME, 1960

England covered in cloud. The control at Benson vectored him in and at 150ft he descended out of the thick cloud to be greeted by the runway dead ahead.

The squadron was yet another that was created solely for the PR role. It was formed at Benson in October 1942 and remained there for the duration of the war and early post-war years. A mixture of aircraft were flown including the Mustang but primarily Spitfires starting with the MK.IV and ending with the Mk.XIX. Naturally, the squadron was tasked with flying missions during Operation Overlord, hence the invasion stripes on PM631.

After the war the squadron was temporarily disbanded but re-formed, first with the Spitfire and later the Meteor, when based in Germany until it disbanded for the final time on September 7, 1957. The Spitfire was then repainted during a winter service in early 2011 again as a 541 Squadron Spitfire though without the invasion stripes or any other codes or markings except for roundels and the serial, as a tribute to the pilots who flew unarmed and alone deep into enemy territory, often failing to return. PM631 has since been absent for several years due to a very thorough and detailed inspection during the scheduled deep maintenance with every inch meticulously inspected. Cracks, misplaced rivets and any other damage, no matter how small has been given attention. Upon completion it will be returned to the same scheme worn when it was first delivered to the Historic Aircraft Flight in 1957.

SUPERMARINE SPITFIRE Mk.XIX PM631

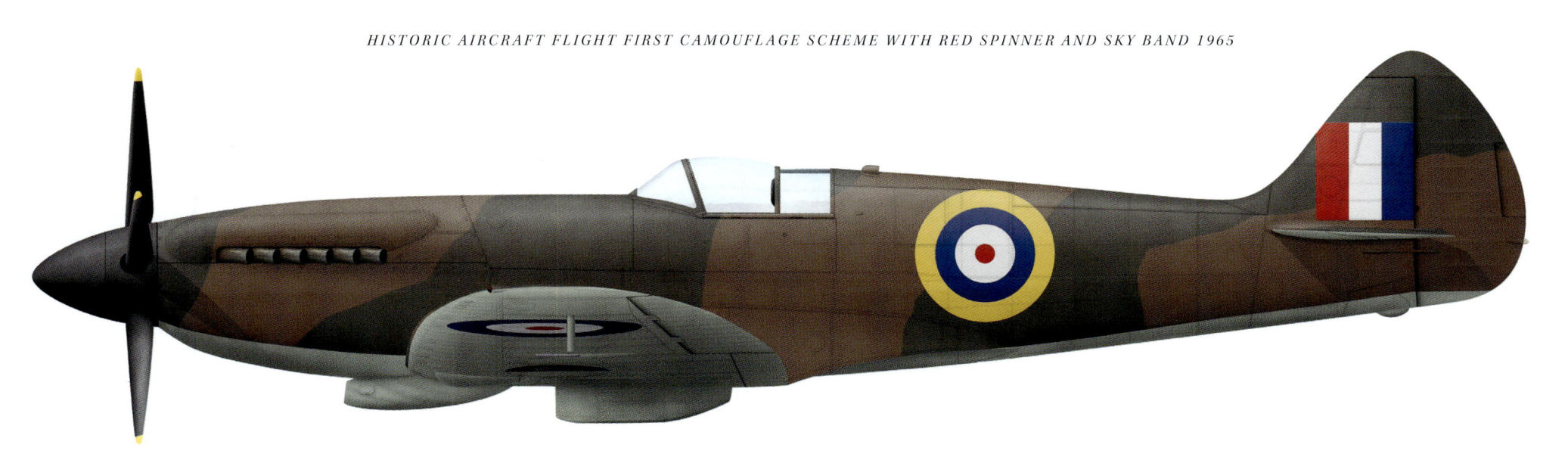

HISTORIC AIRCRAFT FLIGHT FIRST CAMOUFLAGE SCHEME WITH RED SPINNER AND SKY BAND 1965

TEMPORARY APPLIED PRIOR TO BATTLE OF BRITAIN FILMING, 1968

BATTLE OF BRITAIN MEMORIAL FLIGHT IN PROFILE

CD-K N3319 TEMPORARY BATTLE OF BRITAIN FILM SCHEME, 1968

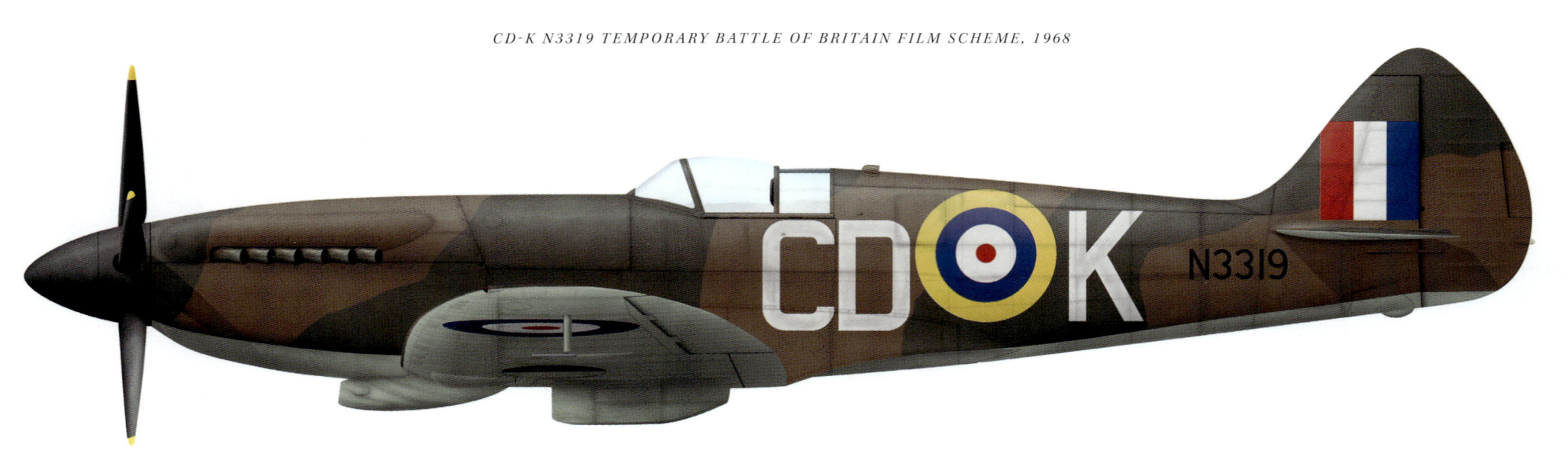

DO-G N3316 TEMPORARY BATTLE OF BRITAIN FILM SCHEME, 1968

SUPERMARINE SPITFIRE Mk.XIX PM631

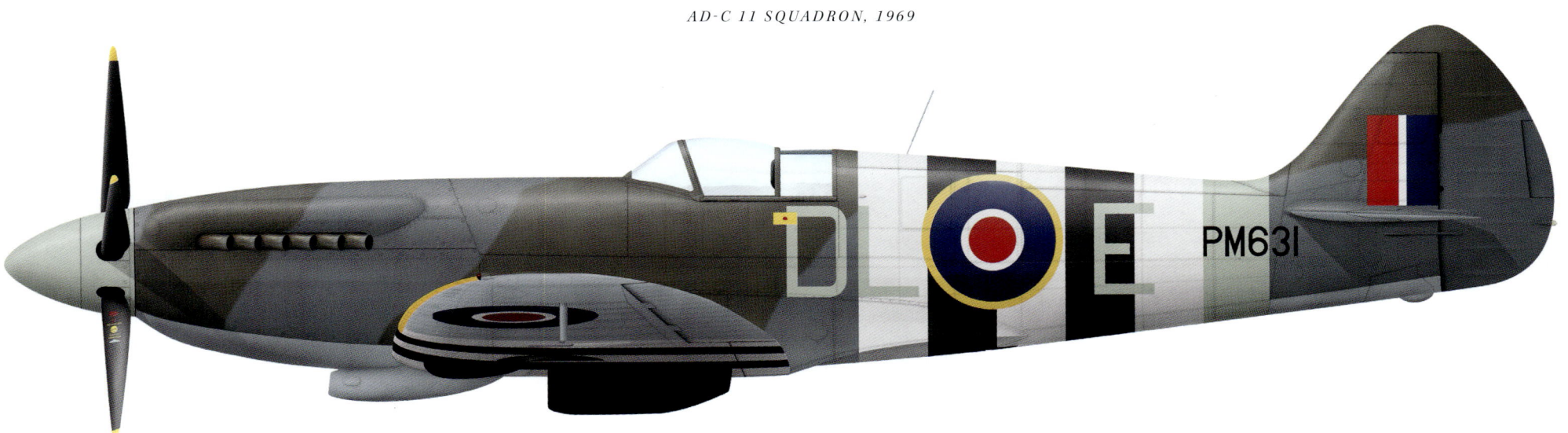

AD-C 11 SQUADRON, 1969

DL-E 91 SQUADRON REPRESENTING LA200, 1984

BATTLE OF BRITAIN MEMORIAL FLIGHT IN PROFILE

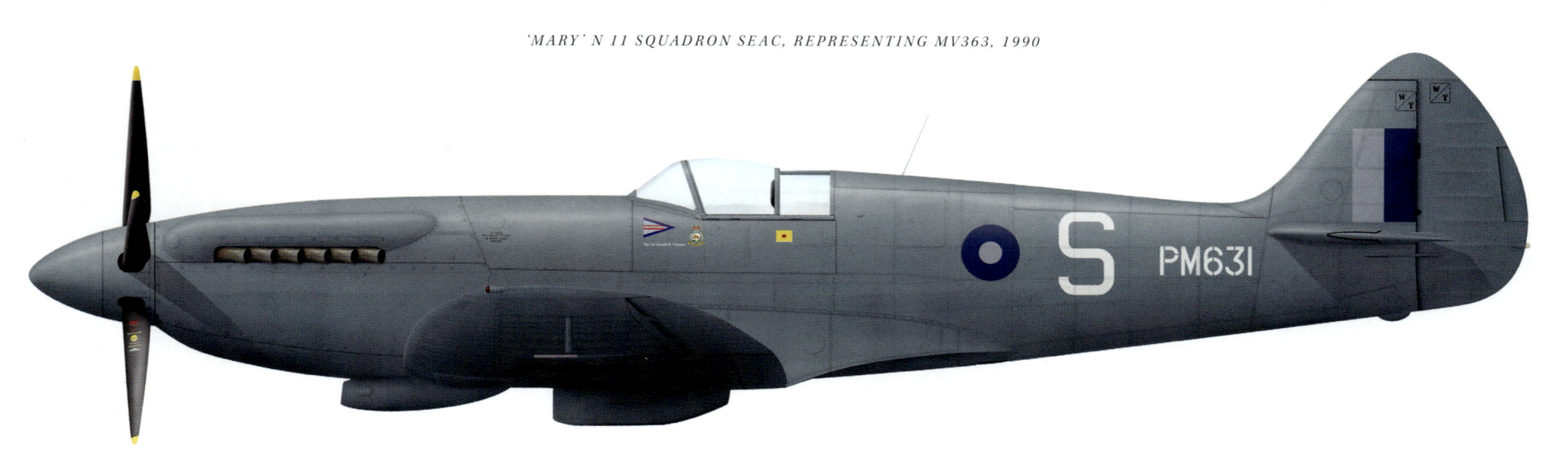

'MARY' N 11 SQUADRON SEAC, REPRESENTING MV363, 1990

S 681 SQUADRON SEAC, 1996

SUPERMARINE SPITFIRE Mk.XIX PM631

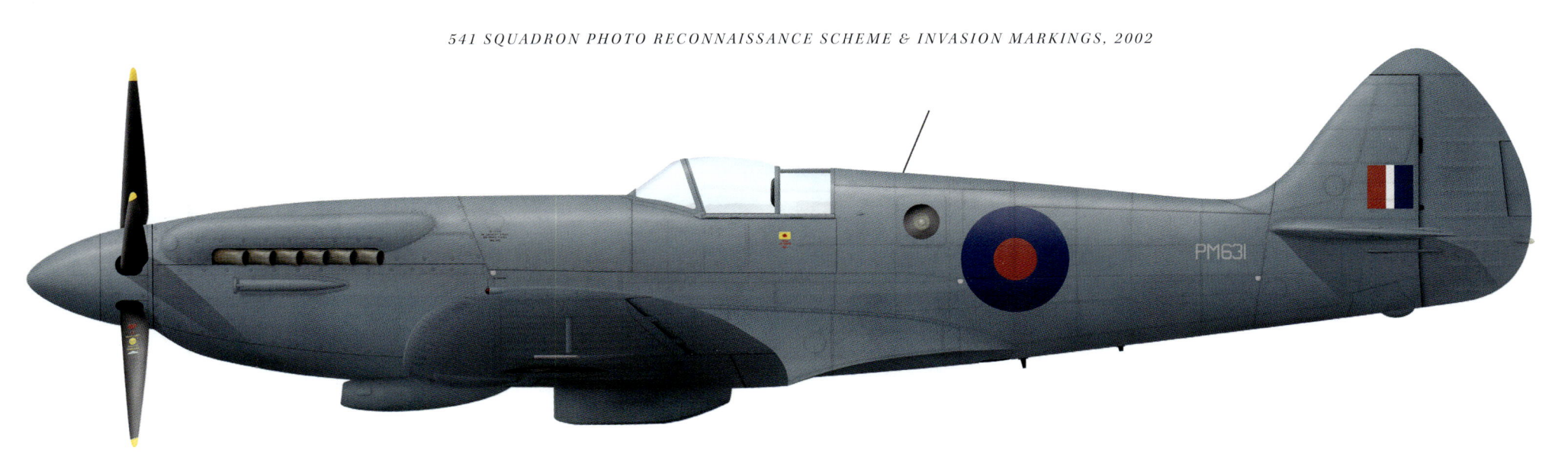

541 SQUADRON PHOTO RECONNAISSANCE SCHEME & INVASION MARKINGS, 2002

514 SQUADRON PHOTO RECONNAISSANCE SCHEME, 2011

BATTLE OF BRITAIN MEMORIAL FLIGHT IN PROFILE

514 SQUADRON PHOTO RECONNAISSANCE SCHEME WITH INVASION STRIPES, 2014

HISTORIC AIRCRAFT FLIGHT DELIVERY SCHEME, 2024

SUPERMARINE SPITFIRE Mk.XIX PM631

BATTLE OF BRITAIN MEMORIAL FLIGHT IN PROFILE

SUPERMARINE SPITFIRE Mk.XIX PM631

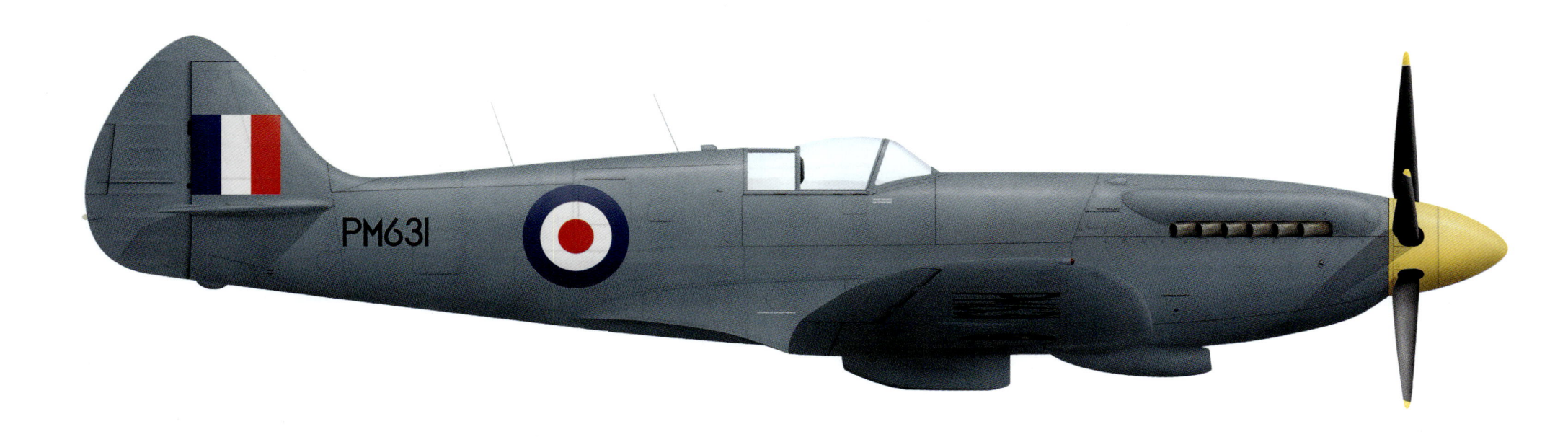

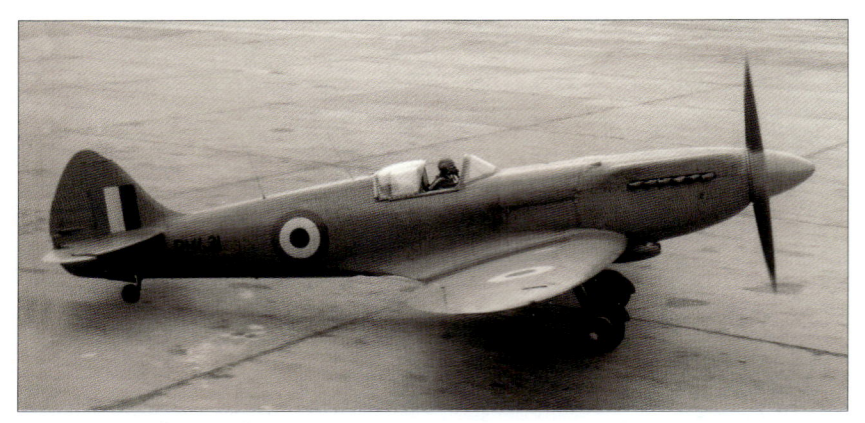

PM631 at Speke Airport whilst with the THUM circa 1956.
PETER ARNOLD COLLECTION

Soon after delivery to the HAF in 1957 PM631 was repainted in Dark Earth and Dark Green. PETER ARNOLD COLLECTION

By the early 1960s PM961 had been repainted with type D1 roundels, the spinner was later changed to red and a sky band was added. DAVID WELCH

PM631 painted in Dark Earth and Dark Green.
RON CRANHAM, PETER ARNOLD COLLECTION

PM631 being taxied by the BBMF CO AVM George Black during the early 1970s.
IAN BLACK

39 years after it had last worn PR Blue PM631 wore it once more when painted to represent a 681 squadron Spitfire, seen here at Duxford in May 1998. PETER ARNOLD

By the 80s the spinner of AD-C had changed to the less conspicuous black.
PETER ARNOLD COLLECTION

PM631 at Cranfield displaying the invasion stripes on the fuselage and upper wings, 1985 PETER ARNOLD COLLECTION

PM631 was in attendance at the very last airshow held at West Malling before it was closed as an airfield and developed in 1992. LES CHATFIELD

PM631 parked outside at Coningsby in August 2008. RICHARD PAVER

As a precaution all Spitfires are weighted down at the tail to save them tipping over; water filled jerry cans are the high tech solution. AUTHOR

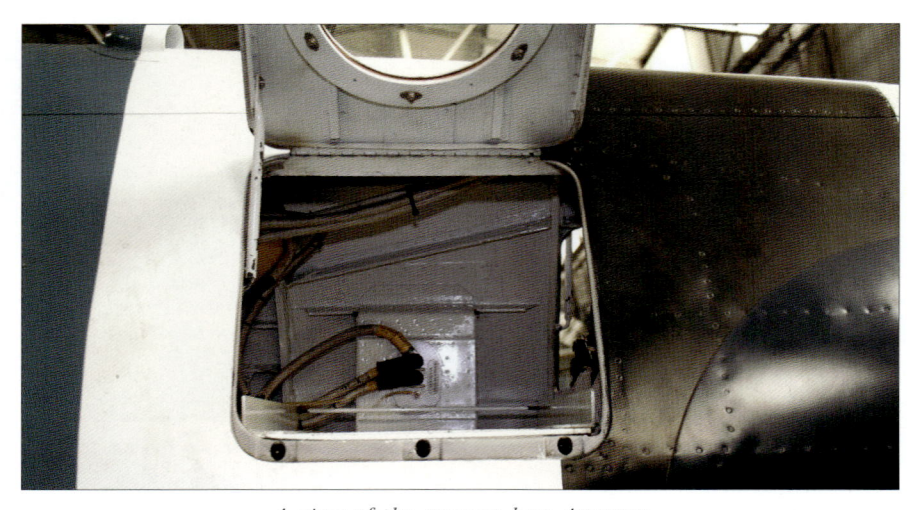

A view of the camera bay. AUTHOR

During the winter of 2017/18 PM631 underwent an extensive overhaul at Coningsby including the removal of the engine. AUTHOR

SUPERMARINE SPITFIRE Mk.XIX PM631

Aerial shot showing the effectiveness of PR Blue against a clear sky.
RICHARD PAVER

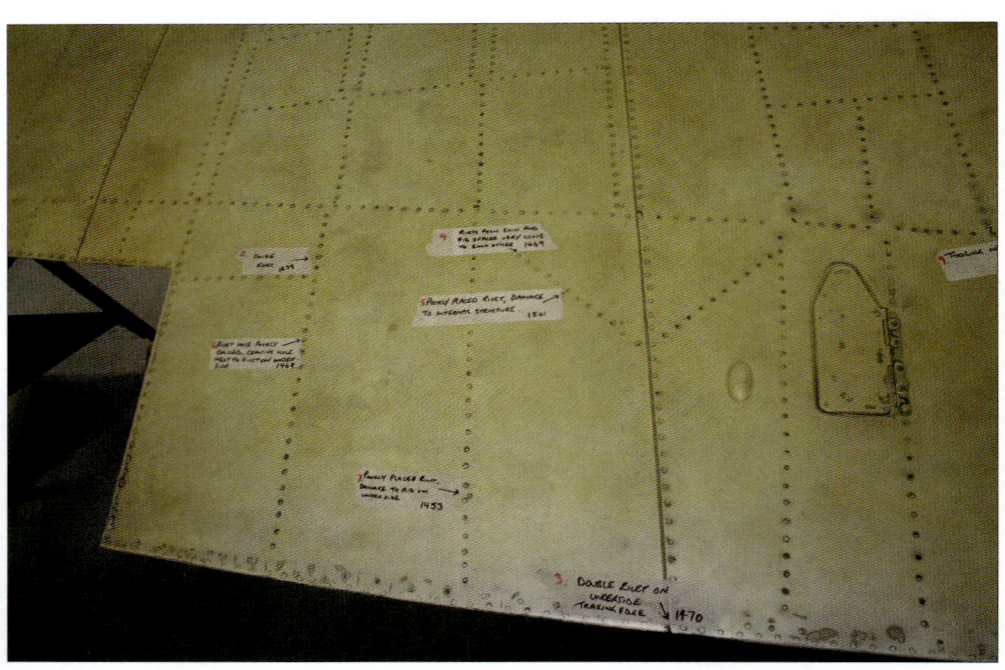

BATTLE OF BRITAIN MEMORIAL FLIGHT IN PROFILE

A meticulous inspection of the airframe highlights many issues including misplaced rivets on the wing that all require attention before PM631 returns to flight. AUTHOR

Stripped down and undergoing deep maintenance. Author

SUPERMARINE SPITFIRE Mk.XIX PM631

PM631 at Coningsby. LISA HARDING

PS915 taking off for a display routine at RIAT, July 2018. Rob Monfea

SUPERMARINE SPITFIRE PR Mk.XIX PS915

Supermarine Spitfire Mk.XIX PS915 was delivered too late to see active service in Europe and, despite being one of the flight's founding aircraft in July 1967, it did not become a flying participant until 1987. It is one of the two Griffon engine Spitfires operated by the BBMF.

Work on the final batch of 79 PR.XIX Spitfires started in 1944 with deliveries beginning in November of that year but the last of these (PS908-PS935) did not make it into service until after VE Day, although PS915, c/n 6S/585121 was officially delivered on April 17, 1945, to 6 Maintenance Unit based at Brize Norton.

Having been moved to Benson on the 26th it was eventually allocated to 514 Sqn, based at Benson, on June 21. In December PS915 became part of No 1 Pilot's Pool until it was acquired in July 1946 by the Photo Reconnaissance Development Unit, also based at Benson, which used it for the testing of new cameras.

It remained as a test aeroplane until July 8, 1948, when PS915 moved to Germany and joined 2 (Army Co-operation) Squadron at Wunsdorf and received the code OI-K. By the summer of 1945 the Second Tactical Air Force had been reorganised as the British Air Force of Occupation and the squadron was tasked with photo reconnaissance across Europe using a mix of Spitfire Mk.XIVs and XIXs in both PR Blue and High Speed Silver. Serials on the PR Blue Spitfires were a mix of white and black but no photographs of PS915 with 2 Sqn have come to light clearly showing what colour the serial was.

PS915 spent a brief period with the BAFO Communication Squadron before joining the THUM (Temperature and HUMidity) Flight at Woodvale, Southport in June 1954. The flight employed civilian pilots who would take a PR.XIX to 30,000ft at 9am daily for barometric measurements. The flight phased out its Spitfires in favour of the Mosquito in 1956 and PS915 then became a founding member of the Historic Aircraft Flight in June 1957 at Biggin Hill.

However, due to the poor condition of its airframe compared

PS915 514 SQUADRON, 1945

to those of the other Spitfires, PS915 spent many years in a variety of schemes exposed to the elements as a gate guardian at various stations until 1984, apart from a brief period as a static in the Battle of Britain film. The locations were: RAF West Malling 1957-1961, RAF Leuchars 1961-1968 and 1969-1975, RAF Brawdy 1975-1977, RAF Coningsby 1975, RAF St Athan 1978-1980 and RAF Brawdy 1980-1984. Some conservation work was undertaken during this period to delay the aircraft's deterioration and further work occurred when PS915 was put back together following the Battle of Britain film. Several parts had been borrowed and used on other Spitfires during the filming. Also, only black and white photographs survive of some schemes, so there has been some speculation on the actual colours due to liberties being taken with the schemes during this period. Commencing in 1984, BAe worked on restoring PS915 in a three-year project at Warton. It was a very thorough process that was not helped by the poor state the Spitfire was in. Birds had been nesting in it, the propeller was close to falling off and it needed a powerplant. In 1977 the BBMF began exploring the feasibility of replacing the Mk.XIX Griffon 66 engine with a Griffon 58 taken from a Shackleton. It was not a simple case of dropping in the new engine though, as the Shackleton had contra-rotating propellers and was a slightly different size.

However, by removing some support lugs and modifications to the rear of the supercharger, PS915 was fitted with a working engine. The work was carried out by Rolls-Royce, which also

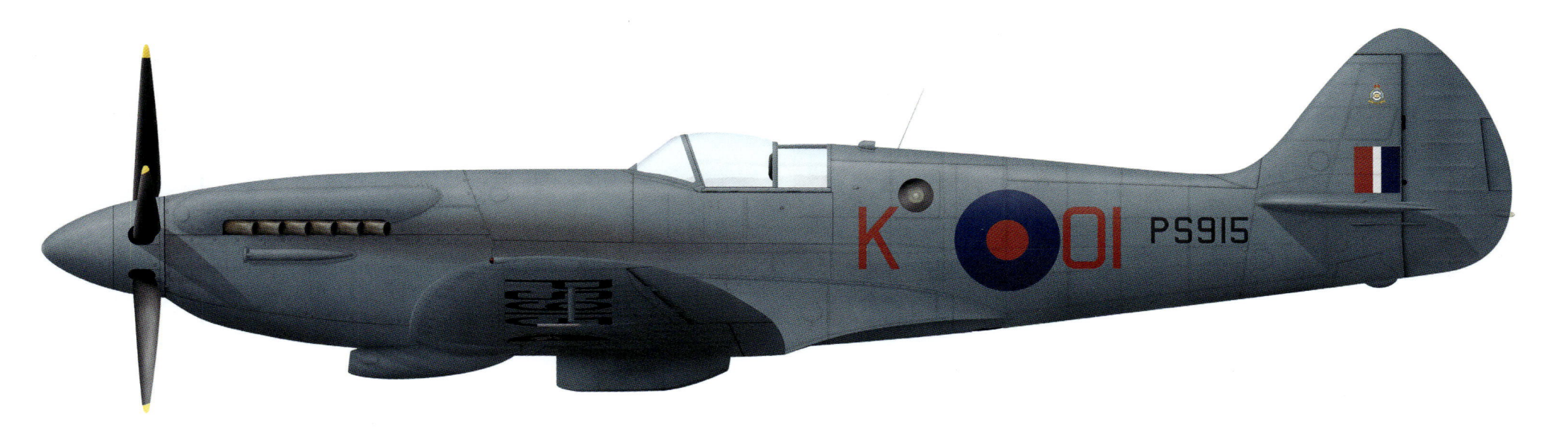

OI-K 2 SQUADRON, 1948

produced seven modified reduction gearboxes to allow the Griffon engine Spitfires to cope with the Griffon 58.

The restoration work was largely completed by November 20, 1986, when PS915 was fired up and, on December 20, Sqn Ldr Paul Day took it up for an air test, the first since it had joined the flight in 1957. Just prior to the first post-restoration flight PS915 was painted in an all over gloss PR Blue scheme, very similar to its original scheme in 1944, but with a smaller serial number. Following further work and tests PS915 was officially returned to the BBMF on April 7, 1987, 30 years after it was first delivered. Having worn this scheme for four years it was repainted over the winter of 1991/92 in a distinctive Dark Earth and Dark Green camouflage with yellow undersides, representing the prototype Spitfire Mk.XIV JF319, a tribute to the work carried out by the test pilots of A&AEE at Boscombe Down and Supermarine during the war.

JF319 was itself a converted Mk.VIII fitted with a Griffon 61 engine, five-blade Rotol propeller and a number of other improvements over the Mk.VIII. It was completed in late June 1943 and sent to A&AEE for extensive testing, including trials against the Bf 109 G and a temporary fitting of a six-bladed contra-rotating Rotol propeller that was prone to failure. It was eventually struck off charge on May 2, 1945. With another service scheduled for the end of the 1997 display season, PS915 was once again repainted with a camouflage scheme, this time in South East Asia Command (SEAC) colours with the revised roundels that omitted the red to avoid confusion with the Hinomaru on Japanese aircraft. The original aircraft used as the basis

TEMPERATURE AND HUMIDITY FLIGHT 1954

for the new scheme was RM908, UM-G that had served with 152 (Hyderabad) Squadron in the Far East during the war. Having originally operated in the Middle East the squadron moved to India in the last weeks of 1943, initially becoming part of Calcutta's defence force but it went on to conduct fighter sweeps over Burma, flying transport and bomber escorts while operating from temporary airfields in the country.

RM908 was built as a Mk.XIV, delivered to 29 MU on March 4, 1945, and shipped to India at the end of the month, arriving with the squadron in May when the squadron codes and leaping black panther were added to the fuselage. It remained with the squadron during the last few months of the war and with a decline in attacks by Japanese aircraft the Spitfires were used for bombing. 152 Sqn moved to Tengah and was temporarily disbanded on March 10, 1946. RM908 was officially struck off charge on February 27, 1947.

PS915 narrowly escaped serious damage or a potential writeoff on July 6, 2002, when there was the distinct possibility of a wheels-up landing due to the gear being stuck. Sqn Ldr Clive Rowley had taken off from Coningsby in PS915 for a display with a Hurricane and the Dakota on the Isle of Man. Following the display, he headed to the local airport at Ronaldsway for an overnight stay and attempted to lower the undercarriage, however, the lever stuck halfway down.

SUPERMARINE SPITFIRE PR Mk.XIX PS915

HISTORIC AIRCRAFT FLIGHT, 1957

An issue with the tail wheel jack ultimately caused a drop in hydraulic pressure so the main wheel up lock pins could not retract. Having tried various manoeuvres including negative G to shake them loose, Rowley faced the distinct possibility of a wheels-up landing but the Dakota was still in the vicinity with a number of BBMF technicians on board, including Cpl Clive O'Connell, who suggested flying inverted straight and level to take the pressure off the pins, allowing them to retract and the wheels to be lowered. Those present at the airfield were witness to a Spitfire Mk.XIX flying inverted at 180kts while lowering its undercarriage. Over the weekend the fault was traced and repaired allowing PS915 to safely return to Coningsby intact.

Having spent several years in camouflage PS915 was repainted in PR Blue during the winter of 2003/4 when the six-year scheduled major service was completed by the Aircraft Restoration Company at Duxford. This time PS888 of 81 Sqn, based at Seletar, Singapore was chosen and it had the particular honour of undertaking the last of several thousand operational missions carried out by an RAF Spitfire. It was also fittingly the 50th anniversary of the event. Inspired by an article he'd seen about the Flight in the national press, Peter Arnold brought up the anniversary during a chance encounter with the then CO of the BBMF, Sqn Ldr Paul Day and Peter offered his services to assist with the research. Details were provided by Brian Rose who was responsible for hastily adding 'THE LAST' to the nose of PS888 shortly after it had returned from the final mission on April 1, 1954,

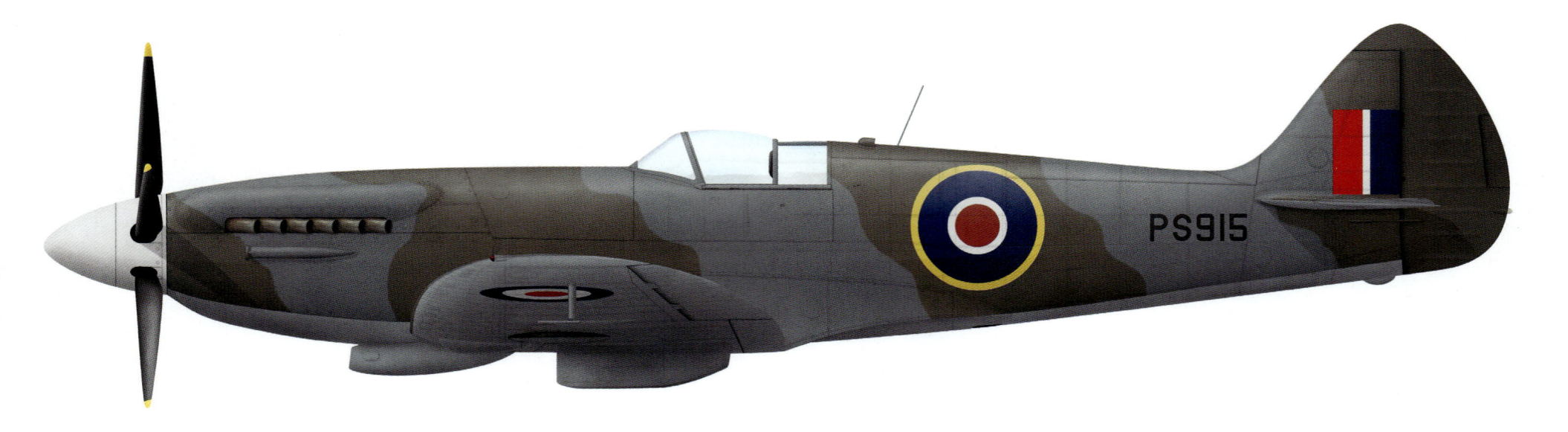

WEST MALLING GATE GUARDIAN, 1957

photographing a suspected guerrilla camp in Johore. Once Sqn Ldr Swaby had landed, the historic event was recorded with the application of the nose art and a brief ceremony.

81 Sqn continued operations with the Meteor and PS888 was passed to the Royal Thai Air Force with whom it became U14-27/97 and went on to be used as an instructional air frame before eventually being scrapped.

PS915 was again repainted following a winter service ready for the 2016 season and once more 81 Sqn was used for the inspiration but this time it was in the High Speed Silver of PS852. On January 1, 1951, two of 81 Squadron's Mk.XIXs (PS852 and PS854) were deployed to RAF Kai Tak, Hong Kong with the intention of flying covert photo-reconnaissance missions over China. These missions were initially flown by Flt Lt Edward 'Ted' Powles and Flt Sgt Padden. The latter being replaced by Flt Sgts Mutch, Hood and Walker.

Powles went on to fly 107 such missions over Chinese territory but it was only during a briefing for his 17th flight that he discovered exactly how secretive they were. He was told that he was not to fly below 30,000ft, that if anything happened to him he was on his own and that neither the British nor the Americans had the authorisation to clear the flights.

For this particular mission he flew to the very limits of the Mk.XIX's range when he was asked to photograph Yulin on Hainan Island, a round trip of 850 nautical miles from Hong

LEUCHARS GATE GUARDIAN, 1967

Kong. The flight lasted three-and-a-half hours and he ran out of fuel, the engine cutting out during his final approach to land, but it was deemed a success by the photographic interpreters.

The detachment also carried out regular meteorological flights over the area and on one such flight Powles managed to set two records, one unintentional and unofficial. Taking off on February 5, 1952, he climbed in PS852 to around 50,000ft (later calculated to be a true altitude of 51,550ft) and set the record for the highest altitude attained by a non-purpose-built piston-engined aeroplane. At this height the pressurised cockpit struggled to cope. Fearing the effects of hypoxia (oxygen deprivation) his only option was a rapid descent to thicker air. Putting PS852 into a dive, the airspeed built up until the controls were reversed, something common when nearing Mach speeds and it was not until he was down to 3000ft that Powles regained control. At the time it was believed that he had reached 690mph or around Mach 0.94 but it is now generally considered an exaggeration of the speed. Despite this, the Spitfire appeared to suffer no damage and the altitude record was recognised.

Of the 225 PR.XIXs built, only four are currently airworthy and three were involved in the formation of the Historic Aircraft Flight: PM631, PS915 and PS853. The last was later sold to raise funds to restore Hurricane LF363 following its crash, which along with PS890 continues to display. The BBMF aircraft are flown as a tribute to the valuable yet frequently dangerous photo reconnaissance missions undertaken during and after the war.

BATTLE OF BRITAIN MEMORIAL FLIGHT IN PROFILE

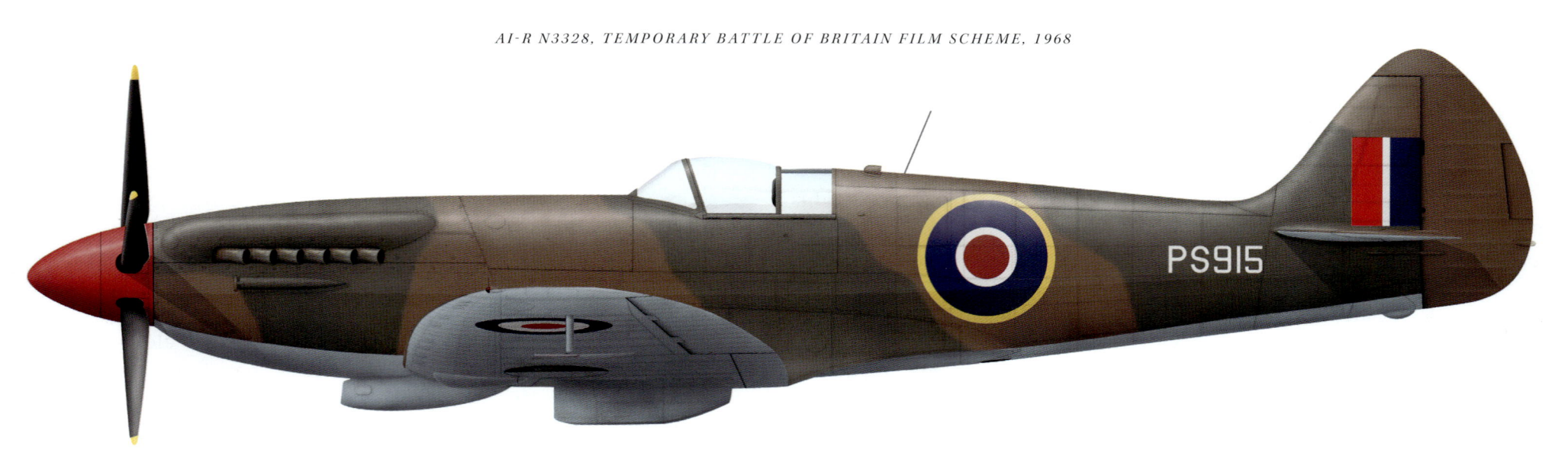

AI-R N3328, TEMPORARY BATTLE OF BRITAIN FILM SCHEME, 1968

LEUCHARS GATE GUARDIAN, 1969

SUPERMARINE SPITFIRE PR Mk.XIX PS915

BRAWDY GATE GUARDIAN 1980

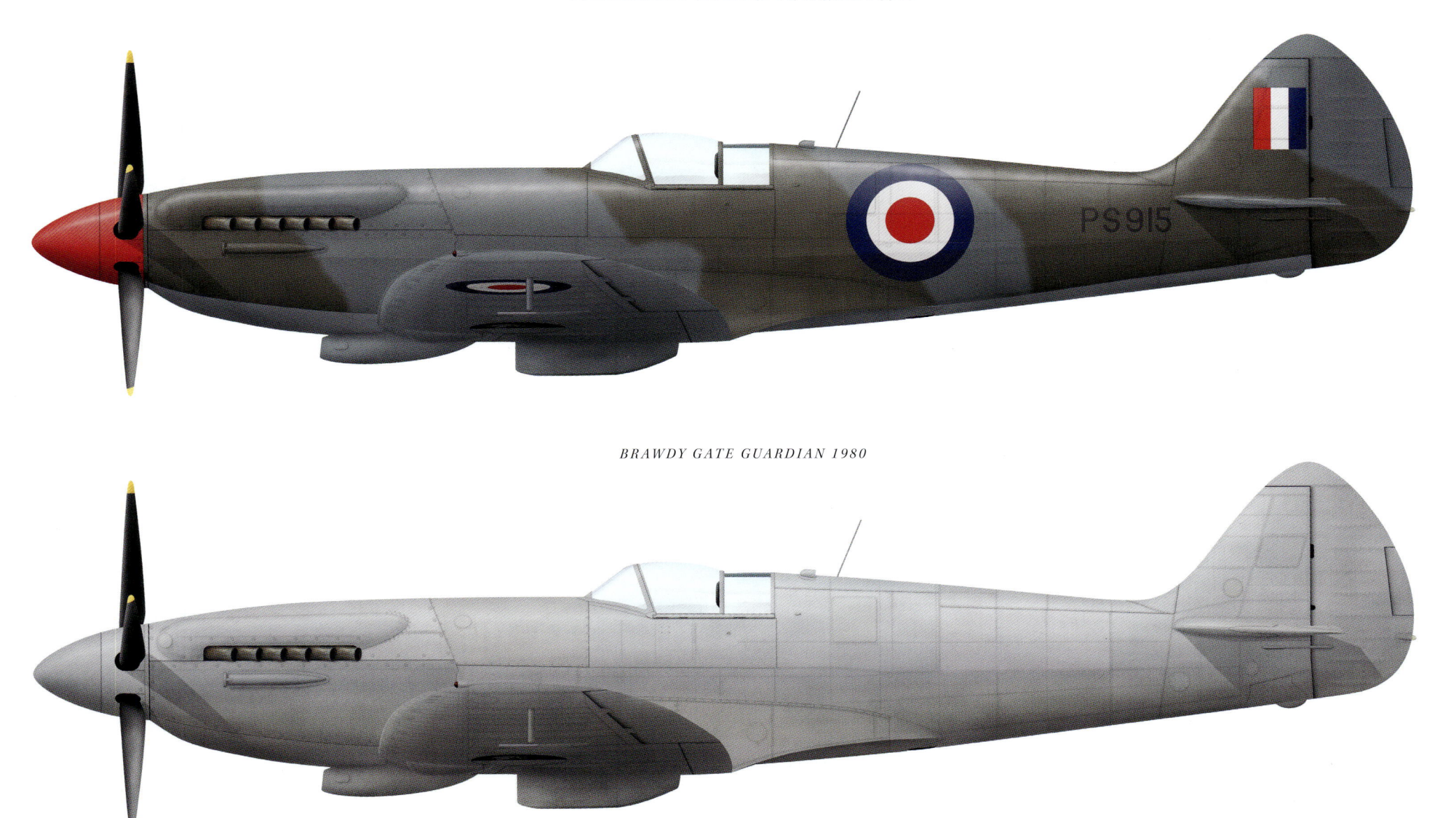

STRIPPED FOR BRITISH AEROSPACE RESTORATION, 1984

BATTLE OF BRITAIN MEMORIAL FLIGHT IN PROFILE

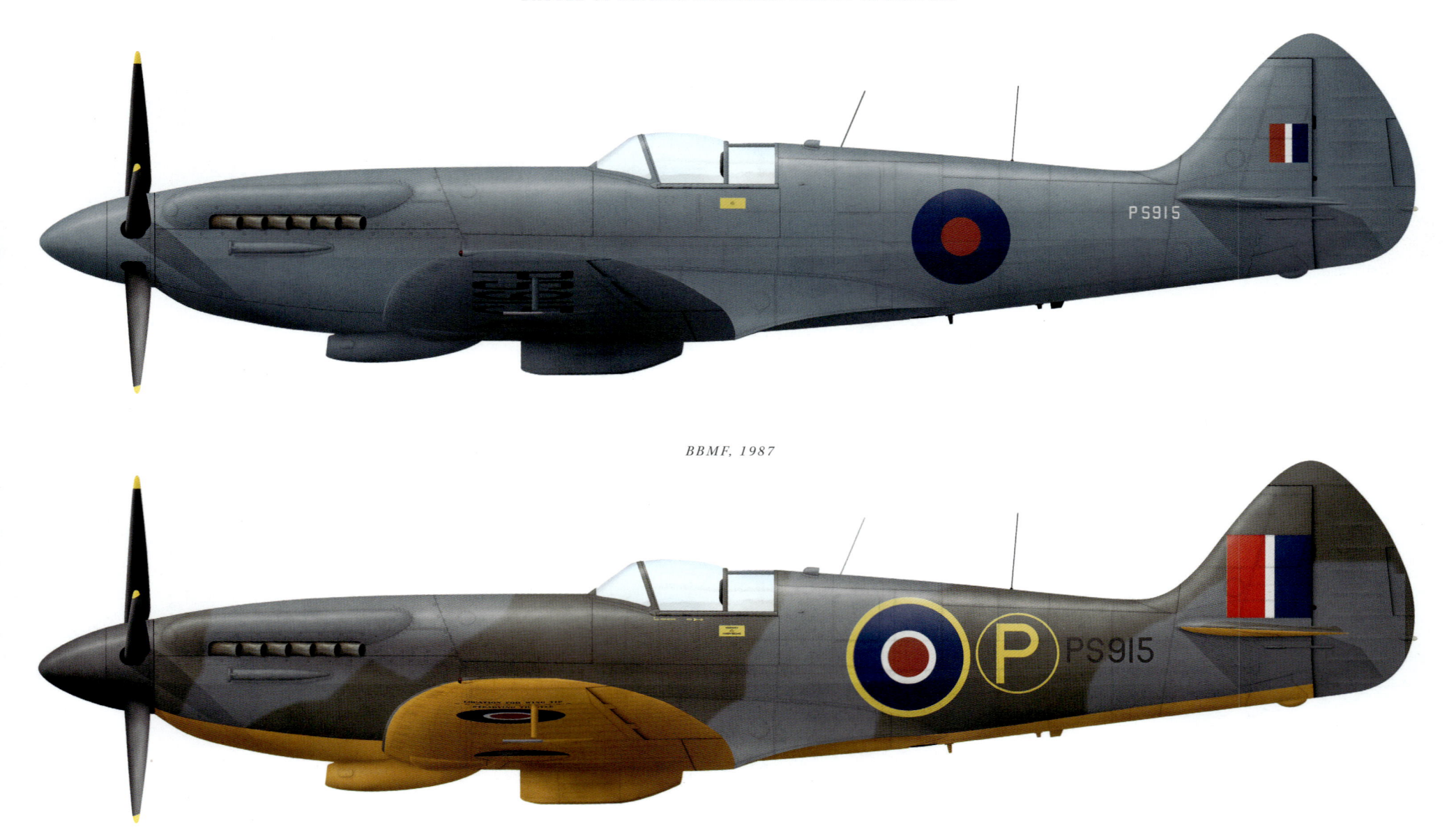

BBMF, 1987

REPRESENTING PROTOTYPE SPITFIRE MK.XIV JF319, 1992

156

SUPERMARINE SPITFIRE PR Mk.XIX PS915

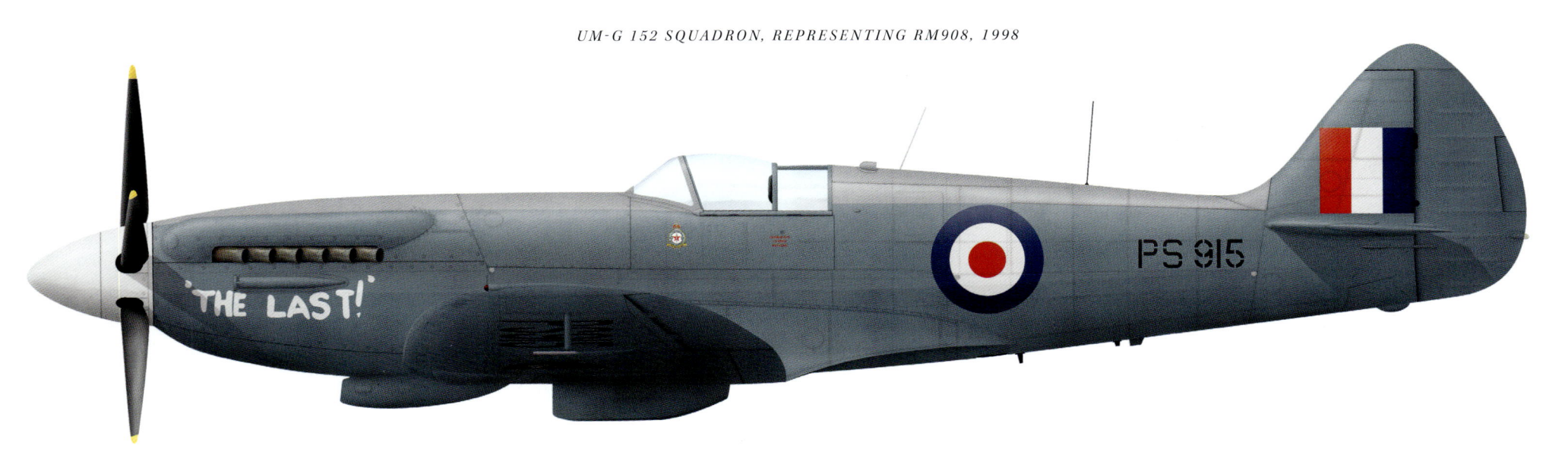

UM-G 152 SQUADRON, REPRESENTING RM908, 1998

'THE LAST' 81 SQUADRON, 2004

BATTLE OF BRITAIN MEMORIAL FLIGHT IN PROFILE

SILVER SCHEME 81 SQUADRON, 2016

SUPERMARINE SPITFIRE PR Mk.XIX PS915

BATTLE OF BRITAIN MEMORIAL FLIGHT IN PROFILE

SUPERMARINE SPITFIRE PR Mk.XIX PS915

BATTLE OF BRITAIN MEMORIAL FLIGHT IN PROFILE

A line up of 2 squadron Spitfires at Wahn, Germany in 1948, it is thought PS915 is one of the Spitfires in the photo. PETER ARNOLD COLLECTION

SUPERMARINE SPITFIRE PR Mk.XIX PS915

Photograph of PS915 at Luneburg, Germany circa 1947. PETER HENDRY PETER ARNOLD COLLECTION

Having completed filming of the Battle of Britain PS915 underwent work to restore it to a suitable condition for the BBMF, 1968. PETER ARNOLD COLLECTION

PS915 on display as a gate guardian at Leuchars in 1962. DAVID WELCH

Once again at Leuchars on static display in a gloss Dark Earth & Dark Green scheme in 1969. MIKE HINES

163

By 1980 PS915 had been painted in a Grey/Green scheme whilst retaining the red spinner. BAE SYSTEMS

In 1984 PS915 was transported by road for a complete rebuild by BAe to flying condition. BAE SYSTEMS

PS915 was fully stripped as part of the restoration process. BAE SYSTEMS

Following the restoration PS915 returned to Coningsby in 1987 and commenced display duties. ANDY CHETWYN

SUPERMARINE SPITFIRE PR Mk.XIX PS915

Taxiing following a display. AD VERCRUIJSSEV

Close up of PS915 in the air. Crown Copyright

Undergoing routine maintenance in August 2011. AUTHOR

PS915's seat removed during winter service. AUTHOR

In the hangar between displays at Coningsby. AUTHOR

The serial can clearly be seen on the lower wings. AD VERCRUIJSSE

PS915 performing a typical fly past during August 2017. GERRY MACHEN

The original 81 Squadron Spitfire flew in bare metal but to protect it from the elements and reduce the risk of corrosion PS915 was painted in an all over aluminium scheme in 2016. CLINT BUDD

Taxiing on a hot summer day at RIAT. ROB MONFEA

Flying in formation with Typhoon ZJ921 of 3 Squadron. CROWN COPYRIGHT

LF363 representing Hurricane V6665, RF-J of 303 (Polish) Squadron. LISA HARDING

HAWKER HURRICANE MK.IIc LF363

LF363 was a founding aircraft of the Battle of Britain Memorial Flight at Biggin Hill in July 1957 when it was joined by three Spitfire Mk.XIXs and the flight was officially formed. Despite a catastrophic crash in 1991, it was rebuilt and continues to fly with the flight's other Hurricane — PZ865.

Several times during the war 63 Squadron was based at RAF Turnhouse (now Edinburgh Airport) including a period from January to May 1944 and it was there that LF363 entered service with the RAF. It was delivered on March 30 when the squadron was going through a transition period from the Mustang I to the Spitfire V. During the war, 63 Sqn was not allocated a squadron code and since the Hurricanes were only with the unit for a few weeks it is unknown what (if any) letter LF363 wore. 63 Sqn had been flying the Mustang in the reconnaissance role so LF363 was fitted with two F.24 cameras. When the squadron moved south to RAF Thruxton, LF363 remained in Scotland, being transferred to 309 (Polish) Squadron at RAF Drem on May 23 and receiving the code WC-F. Again, the Hurricanes replaced Mustangs.

LF363 then followed 63 Sqn south, returning to the unit on November 2 while it was based at RAF North Weald, Essex. By now the squadron had converted to the Spitfire Mk.Vb so it is likely that LF363 was only held there until it was transferred to 26 Sqn, RAF Tangmere, West Sussex at the end of the month. The squadron had been operating Mk.V Spitfires but over the winter it began converting to the Mustang I so the Hurricanes were only an interim replacement. LF363 would have remained with 26 Sqn for only one or two weeks so it may not have been there long enough to have squadron markings applied.

During December 1944, LF363 was allocated to 62 Operational Training Unit at RAF Ouston, Durham, where the four cannon were removed. It stayed with the OTU for the first half of 1945 until it was acquired by Middle Wallop and

63 SQUADRON JANUARY – MAY 1944

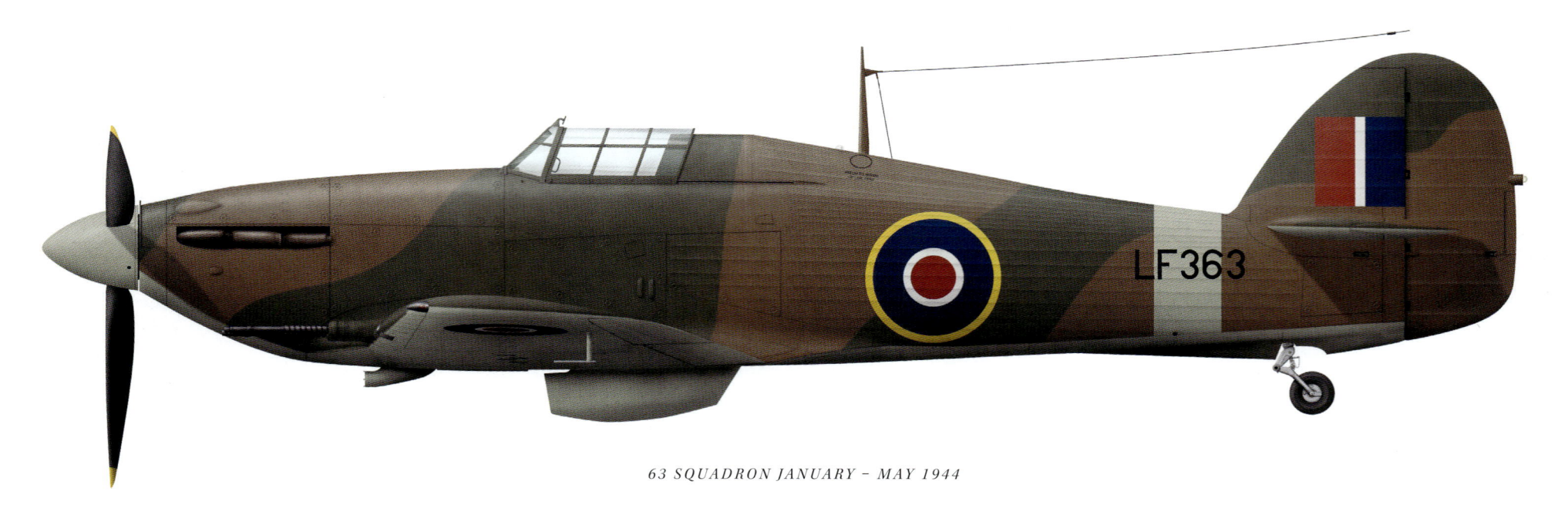

joined the station flight on August 14. There are no details of the markings that LF363 would have worn during this period and to date no photos have come to light. Following the war, records did not tally with the actual movements of LF363 and it was officially struck off charge while still at Middle Wallop, although unofficially it would probably have been used as a hack. It remained there until February 1948 when LF363 moved to RAF Thorney Island's station flight.

Early in 1948 AVM Sir Stanley Vincent DFC AFC commanded 11 Group and requisitioned LF363 as his personal aircraft. Vincent had a very rich and long career with the RAF. Having joined the RFC in 1915, he was posted to 60 Squadron in April 1916 and in July that year he claimed the first victory for the squadron. During the Second World War, he was station commander at RAF Northolt. What makes Vincent's career notable is that he is thought to be the only RAF pilot to have claims in both wars and at Northolt he made seven claims. Vincent had LF363 repainted in Ice Blue with his pennant and the 11 Group crest applied just below the canopy. Following Vincent's retirement in 1950, LF363 was placed in temporary storage until it was re-camouflaged for the film Angels One Five and was one of two Hurricanes (the other being PZ865) which represented 'Septic' P2619 US-B.

Once filming was complete, the Ice Blue scheme was restored

WC-F 309 (POLISH) SQUADRON MAY–NOVEMBER 1944

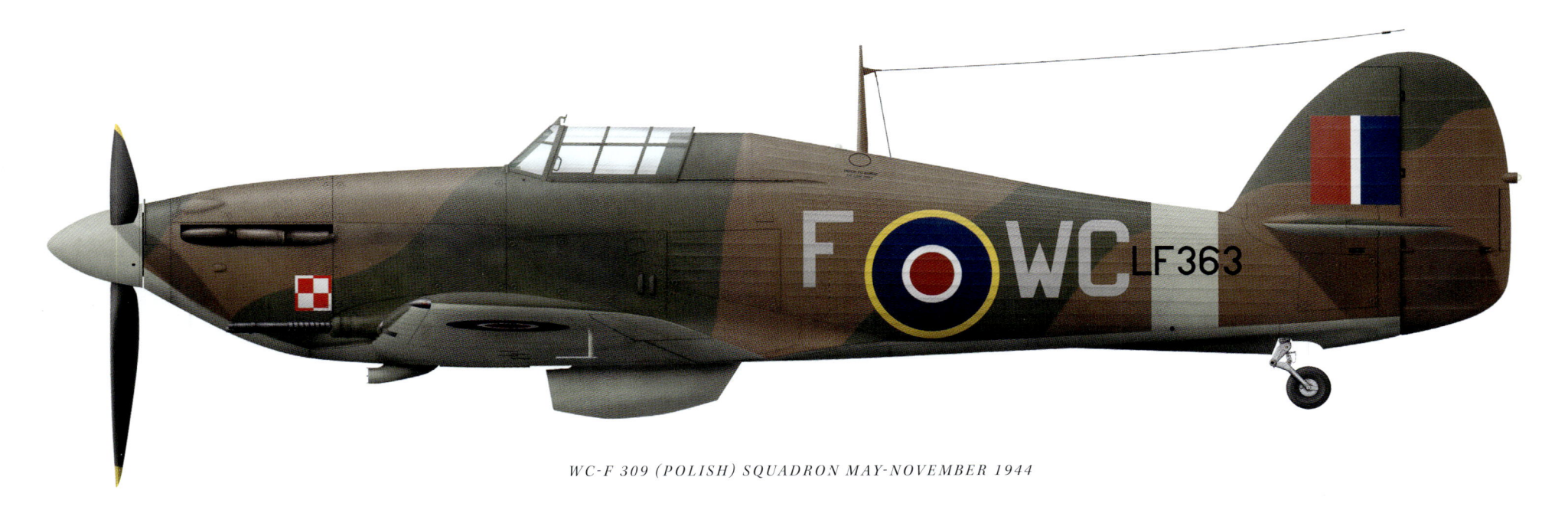

and LF363 ended up at RAF Waterbeach, where it became the last airworthy Hurricane on RAF strength at the time. It was not alone, as Hurricanes LF751, PG539 and Z3687 were also being stored at Waterbeach, and inevitably the three were used as spares to keep LF363 flying. Unsurprisingly, the parts removed from LF363 were not subsequently fitted to the other three and, having been kept in the open, they deteriorated considerably. The Hurricanes were later combined into a single airframe and used as the gate guard at Bentley Priory.

LF363 returned to the silver screen with a role in Reach For The Sky, again receiving a temporary camouflage, along with the serial T4125 and several codes: SD-K, N, R, W and X. Again, the camouflage was removed after filming. It was painted in all over silver and delivered to RAF Biggin Hill, where Group Captain Peter Thompson DFC was station commander. It was Thompson who decided to form the Battle of Britain Memorial Flight in 1957 and LF363 became its founding aeroplane.

During the first few years of the flight, LF363 was painted in a standard Battle of Britain camouflage with just the serial and roundels applied. With the closure of Biggin Hill as an RAF station in 1958, the flight — which by now included several Spitfires — moved to North Weald for a few weeks until that also closed and the flight took up residence at Martlesham Heath, Suffolk.

In 1968, along with every other available Hurricane, LF363 was painted for the Battle of Britain film. Due to it being one of only three

11 GROUP, AVM SIR STANLEY VINCENT 1948-1950

airworthy Hurricanes at the time, it wore a myriad of serials and codes during filming, including codes F, MI-A, MI-D, MI-H and KV-C, and serials H3420, H3421, H3422. LF363 was given a major overhaul once filming was completed and repainted in all over silver once more before being returned to the flight.

For the 1969 display season LF363 wore the first representative scheme when it was painted in the markings of 242 Squadron's LE-D, flown by Douglas Bader. During the war he had flown two LE-Ds — P3061 and V7467 — but unlike the appearances in films LF363's original serial was retained, as all BBMF aircraft have done when wearing representative schemes. The aircraft also had a red tipped spinner and the standard code letters. A couple of years later it was repainted, at which point the code letters were revised with the 'D' in front of the roundel. LF363 continued to fly in this scheme through the majority of the 1970s.

The aircraft was next repainted ready for 1979 in the markings of V7313, GN-F, 249 (Gold Coast) Squadron, flown by Wing Commander Tomas 'Ginger' Neil DFC and Bar. During the war he had a total of 14 kills and his first posting was to 249 Sqn in May 1940. He flew 141 missions during the Battle of Britain.

For the 1983 season, LF363 received a very different scheme when it was painted all over matt black with white codes and red serial to represent a night fighter of 85 Squadron P3118 (probably) VY-X which was based at RAF Gravesend

US-B 'SEPTIC' ANGELS ONE FIVE FILM, 1951

during the winter of 1940-41 and flown by Flt Lt Wheeler. The next change came in 1987 when LF363 returned to the standard early war camouflage of dark green and dark earth, this time in the guise of NV-L, 79 Sqn, and represented a typical aircraft from the Battle of Britain when the squadron was based at Biggin Hill during the height of the battle. LF363 was next painted in the markings of Eric Nicolson's P3576, GN-A of 249 Sqn. Nicholson was the only fighter pilot to be awarded a Victoria Cross during the Second World War and the only VC for action within the British Isles. On August 16, 1940, he was leading a flight of three Hurricanes to intercept a bombing raid. Despite having his Hurricane set alight by some Bf 109s, being shot and suffering burns to his hands, Nicholson remained at the controls to attack a Bf 110 before bailing out.

It would be some years before LF363 would wear another scheme. Having flown for 47 years and avoided any serious incidents during that time, LF363 was practically written off on September 11, 1991. Having departed Coningsby with a Spitfire and the Lancaster for Jersey, the formation was nearing Wittering when the engine stopped running smoothly. The pilot, Sqn Ldr Martin, decided to make an emergency landing at Wittering but during the final approach the engine failed completely, causing LF363 to crash and catch fire. The ensuing fire, made worse by the nearly full fuel tanks for the long flight, destroyed much of the aircraft.

Spitfire PS853 was up for sale three years later to raise funds to

SD-X REACH FOR THE SKY FILM, 1955

restore LF363, which had been languishing at Coningsby. Due to the extent of the damage an almost complete rebuild was undertaken by Historic Flying Ltd and seven years after the crash, on September 29, 1998, it flew again in the markings of 56 Squadron's R4197 US-C, which was flown by P/O Maurice Mounsdon. In US-C, he made seven kills before being shot down over Colchester by Bf 109s on August 31, 1940. 56 Sqn was also an appropriate choice as the badge is a phoenix rising from the flames. They were also based at Coningsby, flying the Tornado F3 in 1998. While still wearing US-C, LF363 suffered a further accident on June 6, 2004, when the starboard undercarriage failed during a landing at Duxford for the 60th anniversary D-Day display, the failure caused it to nose over but the damage was minimal and it was soon returned to the air. AVM Harold 'Birdie' Bird-Wilson's P3878, YB-W of 17 Sqn, was chosen for the next scheme to be applied to LF363 in 2006. Badly burned when he first joined the squadron in 1938, he returned to the unit in April 1940. During the fall of France and the Battle of Britain he made six kills before being shot down in P3878 on September 24 near Chatham. He was the 40th kill for Adolf Galland. Bird-Wilson survived and after a distinguished career he retired from the RAF in 1974. Incidentally, Bird-Wilson's last flight in a Spitfire was shortly before his retirement when he was at the control of the flight's Spitfire P7350.

HAWKER HURRICANE MK.IIc LF363

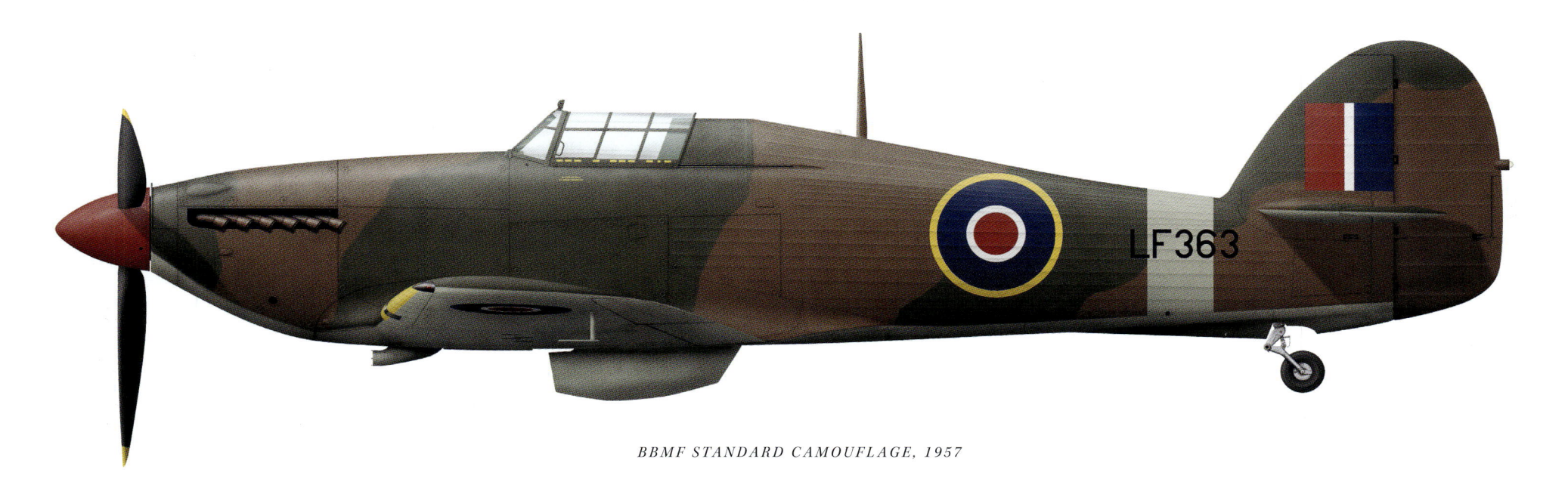

BBMF STANDARD CAMOUFLAGE, 1957

After eight years it was time for another change of scheme. This time P3395, JX-B of 1 Sqn, was picked. It was flown by Flt Lt Arthur 'Darkie' Clowes during the Battle of Britain and over the following winter. JX-B also featured a wasp on the nose and it has been claimed that the stripes on the wasp represented the number of kills he made, but these do not tally up. The wasp and JX-B have since been applied to 1 Squadron's Harrier GR9A ZD403 and the wasp was applied to Typhoon FGR.4 ZK348.

JX-B was replaced with two temporary schemes in 2017. On the port side it once again wore GN-F, but on the starboard side it had the markings of 501 Squadron's SD-A. Although several aircraft wore the code, LF363 represents P2760, which wore the codes during the Battle of Britain when it was primarily flown by Wg Cdr Paul Farnes. He finished the war with eight kills. On September 15, 1940, it was flown by P/O Albert Van Den Hove d'Ertsenryck on his first patrol with the squadron.

P2760 was badly damaged during an engagement with a Bf 109 and the subsequent crash landing attempted by d'Ertsenryck resulted in his death and the aircraft's destruction. The temporary scheme was only intended for the 2017 display season but due to the removal requiring a full repaint the markings remained in place until 2022.

During late 2020 LF363 flew to Biggin Hill where it underwent another scheduled major service. Early on in the service structural damage was discovered. When the fabric around the tail had been

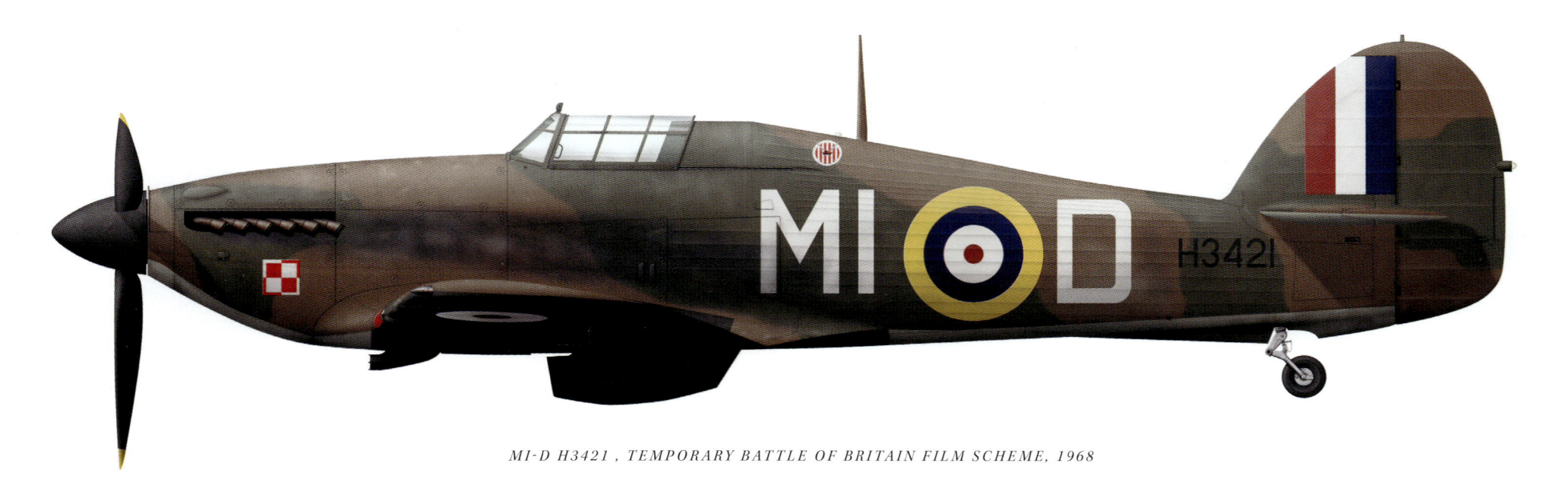

MI-D H3421, TEMPORARY BATTLE OF BRITAIN FILM SCHEME, 1968

removed, it became apparent that there was buckling and corrosion to one of the spars in the tail. Further investigations revealed the severity of the damage, which ultimately necessitated the construction of new replacement spars using modern materials and extended the length of the service. With the service completed and the tail rebuilt, LF363 was repainted and rolled out at the end of February 2022, revealing the new scheme and ready for the forthcoming display season.

The exploits of 303 'Tadeusz Kościuszko Warsaw' Squadron along with the pilots are extensively documented and more than one BBMF aircraft has worn the squadron markings in the past. And it was to the squadron that the flight looked once again for inspiration. This time it was the distinctive scheme of V6665 and the 10½ inch bright red diagonal band that encircled the rear fuselage that was selected.

During the height of the Battle of Britain the fighter units were losing aircraft at a considerable rate and 303 Sqn was no exception. Based at Northolt, the squadron had lost six aircraft with four injured pilots but no fatalities in just one day, the pilots did however claim a total of 38 kills during the fighting, a figure that has since been called into question. The following day, September 7, 1940, the Air Transport Auxiliary managed to replace all the lost aircraft by 10am and among the new deliveries was Hurricane Mk.I V6665. The following day

POST BATTLE OF BRITAIN FILM RESTORATION, 1968

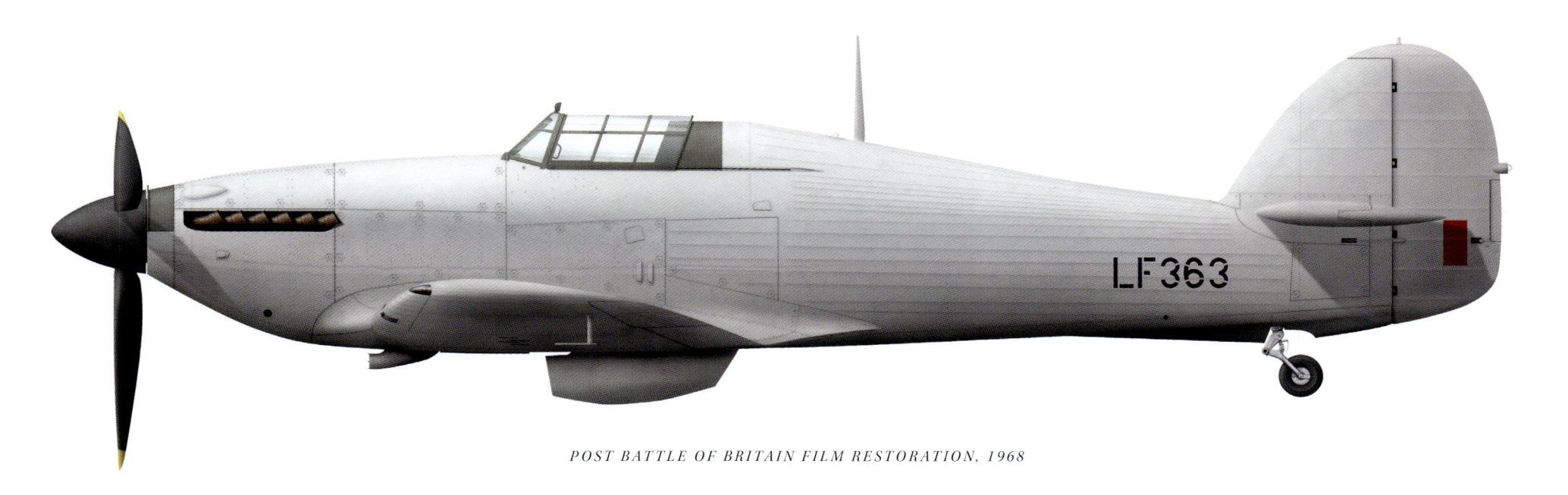

was also a busy day for the squadron, but V6665 was not part of the action, which allowed the ground crew time to apply the code RJ-F, the squadron badge on both the port and starboard sides aft of the canopy along with the band. The reason for the band was an experiment to aid in quick identification of the aircraft within the squadron and it was painted on three aircraft including V6665, but subsequently abandoned.

Flt Lt Johnny Kent flew the Hurricane on its first operational sortie the following day, taking off around 17.00 and leading A Flight on a patrol during which they encountered a formation of 40 to 50 bombers. Kent, accompanied by his wingman Sqn Ldr Zdzislaw Heenenberg, picked a Ju 88 A and attacked, damaging the starboard engine and starting a fire. Kent then lost sight of the aircraft and was unaware of its eventual fate. The damage does match the description of that received by Ju 88 Wn.333 4D+AD of Stab III/ KG30 which crashed at Pagham Harbour, Sussex at 17.50 with the starboard engine and both radiators reported as having been hit, so it is conceivable that this is the aircraft he attacked.

Kent says he then headed in the direction of the French coast, hoping to pick up the damaged bomber again, but he encountered a twin-tail aircraft. His first thought was that it could be a Hampden, but as he closed in, it opened fire. While turning Kent identified it as a Bf 110 and continued to attack until it crashed into the sea ten miles off the coast of Dungeness.

LE-D 242 SQUADRON, 1969

Feeling elated at having gained his first confirmed kill, Kent failed to notice some gentlemen as he taxied in. He then looked to his left, only to witness Air Marshall Dowding and the station commander ducking to avoid being decapitated by the wing of V6665. "Years later I reminded Lord Dowding of the occasion and told him that it had given me the opportunity of saying that I was probably the only fighter pilot in the Battle of Britain to whom the C-in-C bowed as he passed. He rather took the wind out of my sails by saying that he remembered the incident well and that he could think of 'no more noble cause in which to bow!'"

Kent later thanked his wingman, Heenenberg, for keeping the Hun off his tail to which Heenenberg replied: "Not one Messerschmitt — six!" The next three weeks were busy for the squadron and V6665, which was flown by Kent 11 times and a total of 19 times with Sgt Michal Brzezowski claiming two He 111s and Sgt Tadeusz Andruszków a Do 17 on September 26. The following day Andruszków was again in the cockpit of V6665 when the squadron engaged a formation of Bf 109s over Horsham when he was hit and the Hurricane crashed in flames at 9.35 on Holywych Farm, Cowden. Andruszków was buried at Northwood Cemetery and V6665 only lasted 20 days.

The only minor incident of note since LF363 returned to the air has been an undercarriage fault with the port wheel coming down during a flight, forcing LF363 to divert to Brize Norton in July 2022. It transpired that it was a gear issue and was swiftly resolved.

HAWKER HURRICANE MK.IIc LF363

LE-D 242 SQUADRON WITH REVISED MARKINGS, 1970

GN-F 249 SQUADRON REPRESENTING V7313, 1979

VY-X 85 SQUADRON, REPRESENTING P3118, 1983

HAWKER HURRICANE MK.IIc LF363

NV-L 79 SQUADRON, 1987

GN-A 249 SQUADRON, REPRESENTING P3576, 1990

183

BATTLE OF BRITAIN MEMORIAL FLIGHT IN PROFILE

US-C 56 SQUADRON, REPRESENTING R4197, 1998

YB-W 17 SQUADRON, REPRESENTING P3878, 2006

HAWKER HURRICANE MK.IIc LF363

JX-B 1 SQUADRON, REPRESENTING P3395, 2014

GN-F 249 SQUADRON WITH THINNER SERIAL, 2017

BATTLE OF BRITAIN MEMORIAL FLIGHT IN PROFILE

RF-J 303 (POLISH) SQUADRON REPRESENTING V6665, 2021

HAWKER HURRICANE MK.IIc LF363

BATTLE OF BRITAIN MEMORIAL FLIGHT IN PROFILE

HAWKER HURRICANE MK.IIc LF363

LF363 in all over silver scheme. SAN DIEGO AIR & SPACE MUSEUM

LF363 wearing the thicker LE-D code, 1969. IAN POWELL

LF363 displaying later LE-D code, 1970. MARK TAYLOR

Following a landing accident and subsequent fire in 1991 the restoration process began for LF363. ROB EVANS

LF363 being recovered following a landing accident at Duxford, 2004.
James Kightly

BATTLE OF BRITAIN MEMORIAL FLIGHT IN PROFILE

56 Squadron markings, 1998. James Kightly

US-C at RAF Shawbury, 2000. Andrew Thomas

All black night fighter scheme. MARK TAYLOR

LF363 with earlier thick GN-F code. SAN DIEGO AIR & SPACE MUSEUM

YB-W showing the leading edge camouflage line. TONY HISGETT

YB-W showing personal markings of Bird Wilson. TONY HISGETT

Clowes' Wasp is clearly visible on JX-B. Tim Spouge

LF363 undergoing winter maintenance at Coningsby 2014. Author

The internal structure on show during winter maintenance at Coningsby 2014. Author

17. *Following a major service LF363 is prepared for the application of a new scheme.* BBMF

LF363 flying in formation with Spitfire P7350 and the Lancaster at Flying Legends, Duxford, 2010. Author

The Merlin engine removed during servicing. AUTHOR

LF363 flying with Spitfire XVI TE476, Hawker Hunter F.6 XF511 and Gloster Javelin FAW.7 XH958 of 23 Squadron during 1959. BBMF

Photographed with P.1127 XP831 at Dunsfold; presumably the white rudder is for visibility purposes. KEN ELLIS

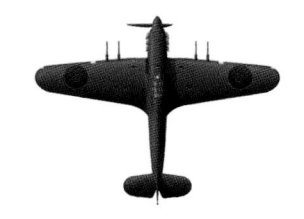

HAWKER HURRICANE MK.IIc PZ865

PZ865 has historic provenance — it was the final Hurricane to be constructed by Hawker and 28 years later the last Hurricane to be delivered to the RAF and enter military service when it was donated to the BBMF.

Construction of PZ865 took place during the summer of 1944 where it was built to the Mk.IIc configuration, with the capacity for four 20mm Hispano Mk.II cannon to be fitted.

As the last of more than 14,500 to be produced, PZ865 was singled out from the beginning with banners celebrating the achievements of the Hurricane around the globe during the war hanging above the last example.

During late July, PZ865 took off from Langley for its maiden flight with P W S 'George' Bulman, Hawker's chief test pilot, at the controls. Fittingly, Bulman had also been at the controls of K5083, the prototype on November 6, 1936, for its maiden flight. During the following month it was named The Last of the Many— a name that has been worn on many occasions over the years. PZ865 was retained by Hawker and used for communications by the company until December 1945.

Placed into storage for the next five years, it was brought out again and converted to a civilian racer configuration with the cannon and aerial removed and the exhaust stubs changed for six individual ones. PZ865 was given the serial G-AMAU which, along with cheat lines, was applied in gold over Oxford Blue. During a major overhaul at Duxford in 2013 some of this original paint was uncovered.

During the 1950s, G-AMAU competed in several air races and, along with a Tomtit and Hart, also in company Oxford Blue with gold, appeared at displays around the country. During 1951 it wore earth and spinach (dark green) for the film Angels One Five, also at the time called Hawks In The Sun, along with LF363, both wearing the same code at different times during filming. Having had the cannon and aerial removed, it is easy to pick out in the film. Once filming was complete it was returned to the racing scheme.

'THE LAST OF THE MANY' WITH ORIGINAL CANNON, 1944

The 1960s saw a return to the ocean grey and dark green scheme along with a new purpose for G-AMAU as a workhorse for Hawker — it was used as a target tug for the company Sea Furies before taking on an altogether more interesting role. The mid-to-late 50s saw a serious attempt to produce a viable V/STOL aircraft and, utilising the Pegasus engine, Hawker produced the P.1127, which would evolve into the Harrier.

G-AMAU was slow enough to act as a chase plane for the P.1127 during transitions to and from vertical to horizontal flight, and the log book shows it was frequently flown by Hawker test pilot Bill Bedford during 1961 and 1962.

Once again, G-AMAU was required for film work— this time the classic Battle of Britain movie. With only three Hurricanes airworthy at the time, it wore a variety of codes and serials. These included the codes H, MI-CMI-D, MI-G, KV-A, KV-M, OK-I and the serials H3421, H3423, H3424. An aerial was also fitted but at an angle which makes it easy to pick PZ865 out. With filming complete in early October, G-AMAU was given a complete overhaul and repainted in late wartime colours. It also wore both the serial PZ865 and the civilian code G-AMAU discretely under the tail.

G-AMAU continued to appear at air displays, flown by the company test pilots for the next two years until the decision was taken to donate the Hurricane, along with the Hart and Cygnet,

G-AMAU 1950-1960

to Hendon. Due to its excellent condition there were individuals high up who believed that G-AMAU should remain airworthy and the best possible place for that was in the hands of the BBMF.

On March 21, 1972, John Farley took it on a test flight to Dunsfold and shortly afterwards permission was granted to hand it over. Duncan Simpson took the initiative and delivered it to Coltishall, where the BBMF was then based, on March 29 before anyone could change their minds. Upon arrival he taxied up to the hangar, shut down the Merlin and was met by a flight sergeant who, according to Duncan, said: "Afternoon sir, what have we here?"

Duncan replied: "It's a Hurricane, flight sergeant — a very special Hurricane — and I'm handing it over to you. Look after it and make sure it's flying right into the future so that future generations can see it." He also said that he expected to catch a bus back but fortunately he was flown back to Dunsfold.

So, 28 years after it first flew, the last Hurricane to be built became the last Hurricane to be delivered to the Royal Air Force. With it being on the military register the civilian code was rescinded and the serial PZ865 could officially be used. This coincided with the first of many repaints PZ865 would receive that would represent other aircraft — the first scheme being that of V6555 DT-A of 257 Squadron, flown by Wg Cdr Bob Stanford Tuck who, by the end of the war, claimed 29 destroyed, two shared, six probable, six damaged and one shared damaged. V6555 was the first of two aircraft to have the code DT-A

US-B 'SEPTIC' ANGELS ONE FIVE FILM, 1951

and be flown by him upon taking command of 257 Sqn in September 1940.

For the 1978 season PZ865 was repainted to represent one of the aircraft of 111 Sqn, the first to receive the Hurricane when it entered service in December 1937 at Northolt. Initially the squadron aircraft had a large 111 on the fuselage; this was replaced with the code TM but with the outbreak of war it was changed to JU, of which JU-Q was a typical example.

It was once again returned to its The Last of the Many scheme in 1982 and wore this for several years until 1989 when PZ865 was painted as RF-U of 303 Sqn, representing R4175 flown by Sgt Josef František, a Czech flying with the Polish squadron who was the highest scoring non-British Allied pilot during the Battle of Britain with a tally of 17 and one probable, all made during September 1940. Due to his unorthodox approach to flying, František never really fitted in with squadron tactics and the eventual solution was to allocate him a 'spare' aircraft and allow him to fly solo patrols as a 'guest' of the squadron. He died on October 8 when his Hurricane crashed in Ewell, Surrey, while returning from a patrol.

Two years later PZ865 was painted in the desert colours of 261 Squadron's P3731, a Mk.I Trop flown by Sgt F N Robertson, based in Malta. The original was part of 418 Flight that consisted of 12 Hurricanes and was delivered to the island by HMS *Argus*

HAWKER COMPANY PLANE 1968-1972

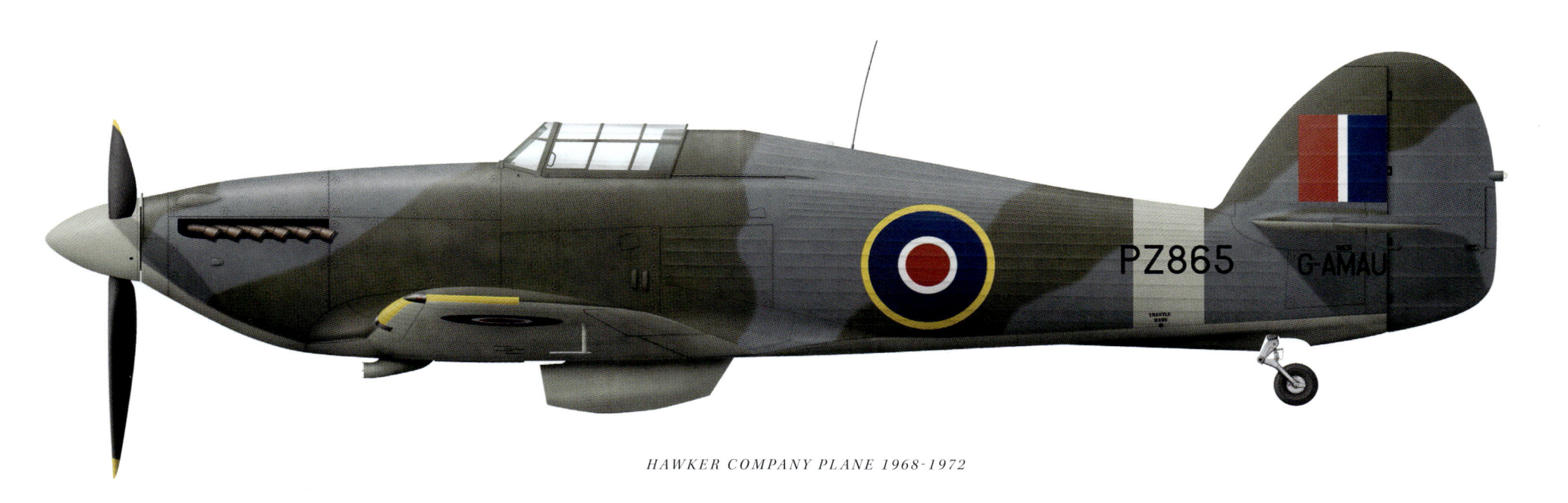

turning point in the Far East campaign following the Japanese defeat. The Hurricanes of 34 Sqn provided close air support throughout the battle, attacking ground targets with their 20mm cannon and two 250lb bombs. On the 18th he led six Hurricanes to attack a bunker that had been proving difficult to destroy.

Flying low, both he and his wingman dropped their bombs — but while pulling out his wingman Jack Morton saw Whalen's Hurricane lazily roll over and plunge into the jungle. Due to technical issues Whalen was not flying EG-S, instead he was in EG-X, LB780. Following his death the nose art panel was removed and later returned to the Whalen family.

The next scheme was a first for PZ865. Although LF363 had been painted in night fighter matt black for the 1983 display season, it had been many years since the flight had paid tribute to the Hurricane pilots that had taken off into the dark skies night after night to hunt for trade. As with all the BBMF schemes, the decision was made a year in advance of the first flight in the new markings and was announced in January 2020. Following the major service the new all-black PZ865 returned to Coningsby on May 5, 2021.

Having been disbanded at the end of WWI, 247 Sqn was re-formed on August 1, 1940 with the Gloster Gladiator at RAF Roborough, Plymouth and tasked with defending the South West. Despite their best efforts the older biplanes failed to locate the monoplanes of the Luftwaffe. Hurricanes began arriving by December 1940, but the

DT-A 257 SQUADRON, REPRESENTING V6555, 1972

success rate was still low. An He 111 was intercepted on April 1 but was lost in cloud, a Fw 200 was also intercepted but only claimed as a damaged, with the squadron having to wait until July 7, 1941 for their first kill, when a Ju 88 A was claimed by P/O Ken Mackenzie. The only Ju 88 loss reported for that night by the Luftwaffe was Ju 88 A-5 3D+BL of 3/KG30, which failed to return from a raid on Southampton.

In June 1941 the squadron became the first to take up residence at the recently constructed RAF Predannack on the Lizard peninsula in south west Cornwall. It was to Predannack that Hurricane IIc BE634 was delivered in January 1942. Constructed at Brooklands, it was taken on charge on October 29, 1941 and evidently took some time to be allocated to 247 Sqn. Upon arrival it was repainted all over in the night fighter black and the code ZY-V applied in red.

An addition to the scheme, BE634 was fitted with anti-glare panels, the purpose to hide the bright flames from the exhaust stubs and preserve the pilot's night vision and this modification was also fitted to PZ865 for accuracy. The 45 gallon drop tanks that allowed the squadron to conduct long range night intruder patrols over northern France were not fitted to the BBMF Hurricane, although they would be an interesting addition.

HAWKER HURRICANE MK.IIc PZ865

JU-Q 111 SQUADRON, 1978

The squadron's Canadian CO, Sqn Ldr Peter O'Brian, chose BE643 as his preferred Hurricane and he is recorded as having flown it on up to three or four sorties in a 24-hour period. While primarily a night fighter unit, the squadron undertook a range of roles, intercepting aircraft during the day, patrols at both dawn and dusk and escorting convoys passing through the English Channel. They also flew in conjunction with Havocs, which were fitted with massive Turbinlite lamps in their noses.

BE643 remained with 247 Sqn until September 8, 1942 when it was transferred to the newly formed 536 Squadron, which was to fly a mix of Turbinlite Havocs and Hurricanes from Predannack. The squadron was disbanded on January 25, 1943. BE643 was eventually struck off charge on December 11, 1944.

The BBMF CO at the time, Sqn Ldr Mark 'Disco' Discombe, selected the scheme to commemorate all the pilots of Hurricane night fighter squadrons who bravely and stoically tried to defend the UK against nightly bombing raids while trying to protect the RAF bomber crews from Luftwaffe night intruders. In particular it is a tribute to the pilots of 247 Sqn and the 16 pilots who lost their lives between February 1941 and December 1942.

BATTLE OF BRITAIN MEMORIAL FLIGHT IN PROFILE

RF-U 303 POLISH SQUADRON, REPRESENTING P3975, 1988

J 261 SQUADRON, REPRESENTING P3731, 1992

HAWKER HURRICANE MK.IIc PZ865

Q 5 SQUADRON, 1998

JX-E 'NIGHT REAPER' 1 SQUADRON, REPRESENTING BE581, 2005

BATTLE OF BRITAIN MEMORIAL FLIGHT IN PROFILE

EG-S 34 SQUADRON, REPRESENTING HW840, 2012

ZY-V 247 SQUADRON, REPRESENTING BE64, 2020

210

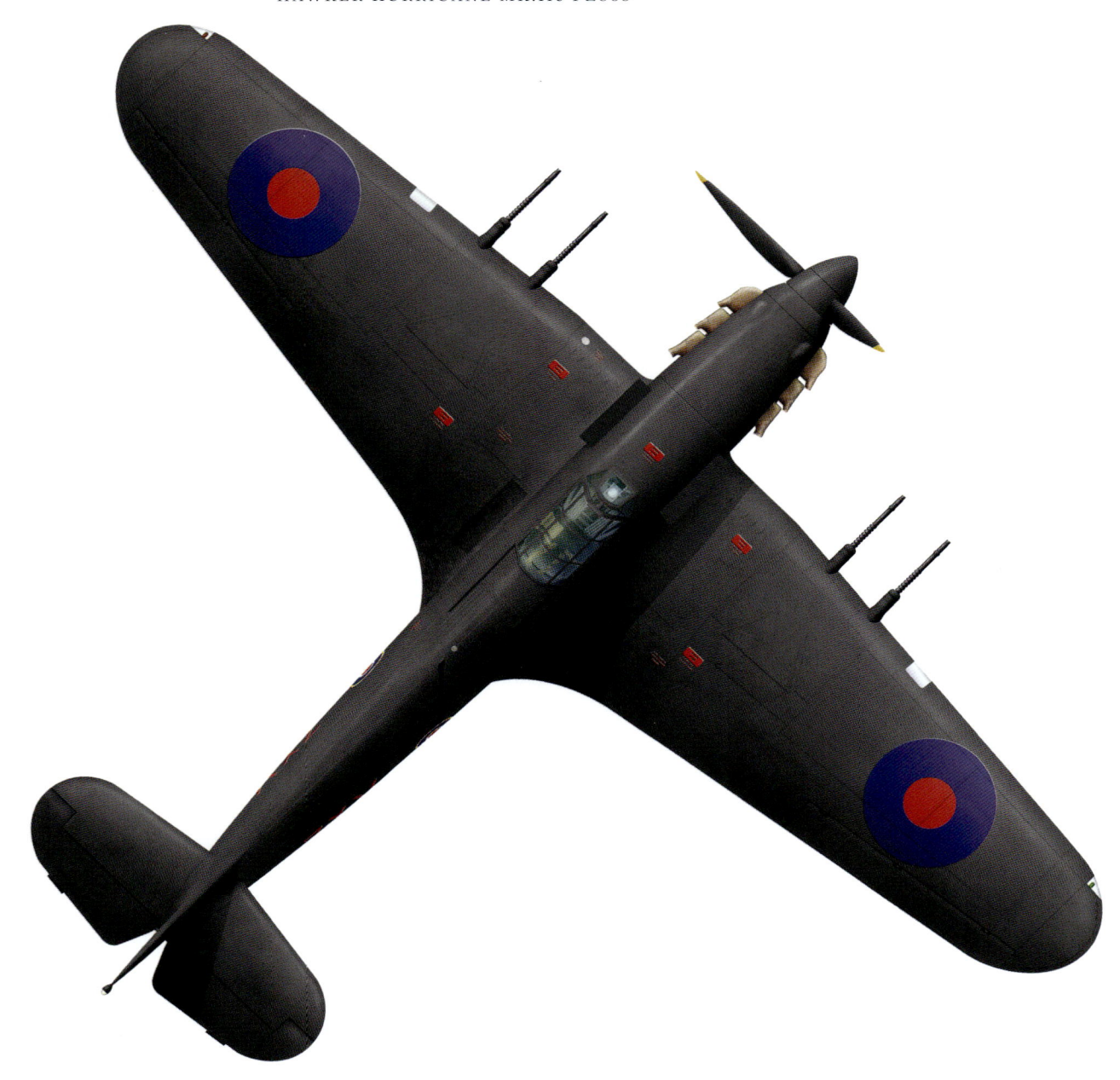

HAWKER HURRICANE MK.IIc PZ865

BATTLE OF BRITAIN MEMORIAL FLIGHT IN PROFILE

HAWKER HURRICANE MK.IIc PZ865

Work on PZ865 fuselage at Langley. BAE Systems

PZ865 having been completed and rolled out. BAE Systems

PZ865 in the civilian scheme as G-AMAU during the 1940s. BBMF

The second time 'The Last of the Many' was painted in camouflage during the 1960s. BAE Systems

HAWKER HURRICANE MK.IIc PZ865

The black & white underside scheme is clearly visible as PZ865 performs a flypast. AD VERCRUIJSSE

Wearing the desert scheme PZ865 taxis at Wroughton in June 1994.
ANDREW READ

JU-Q parked at Biggin Hill.
IAN POWELL

'The Last of the Many' wearing the scheme during the 1982-1987 seasons.
JAMES KIGHTLY

JX-E 'Night Reaper' performing a flypast at Upper Inglesham in July 2009.
RONNIE MACDONALD

PZ865 taxiing out at Coningsby in 2015. CROWN COPYRIGHT

The white bands on the upper surfaces clearly visible as EG-S banks.
JIM CALLOW

PZ865 internal details. AUTHOR

BATTLE OF BRITAIN MEMORIAL FLIGHT IN PROFILE

*Wearing the all black night fighter scheme of 247 Squadron,
PZ865 performs a flypast.* LISA HARDING

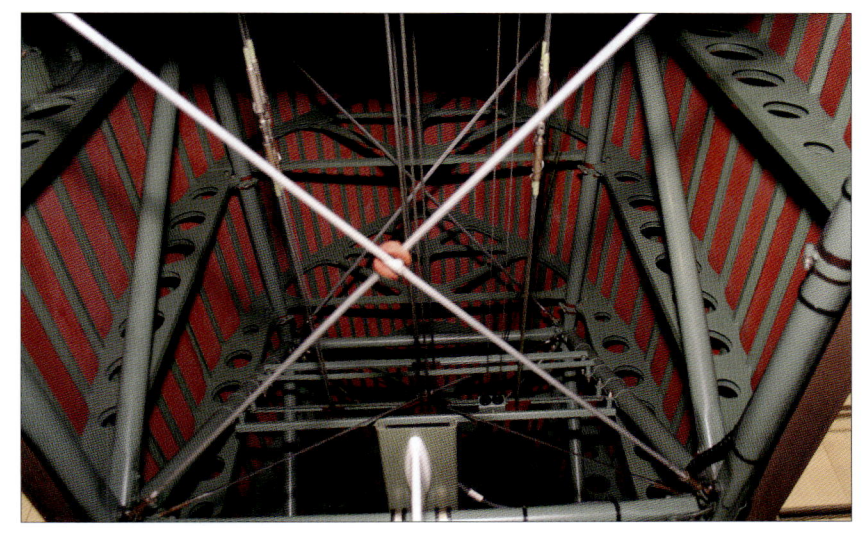

The bracing wires and tubular structure of the Hurricane. AUTHOR

Stripped down during the annual winter service. AUTHOR

Detail of Whalen's nose art on EG-S. AUTHOR

An interesting comparison of the wing tips of PZ865 and Spitfire MK356. AUTHOR

Performing a formation take off with MK356. LISA HARDING

PZ865 *in flight.* CROWN COPYRIGHT

'Thumper' during a night engine test at Coningsby, 2013.
CROWN COPYRIGHT

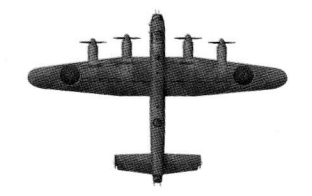

AVRO LANCASTER B Mk.I PA474

Produced in greater numbers than the Halifax or Stirling, the iconic Lancaster is the most well-known of the three heavies. Several airframes survive but only two are currently airworthy. PA474 is operated by the BBMF as a flying tribute to all those crews who lost their lives flying with Bomber Command during the war.

Work commenced on PA474 late in the war but it was not completed until May 31, 1945, three weeks after VE day. It was built at Broughton, North Wales, one of Vickers-Armstrong's shadow factories. Despite there being no need for more bombers in Europe, it was assumed that the war in the Far East could go on for months if not years with the invasion of the Japanese mainland anticipated. At the time the atomic bombs were top secret and it was not even known what effect they would have on the war, so Tiger Force continued preparing for the pending operation.

To operate in the tropical conditions some modifications were required, so slightly larger radiators and intakes were fitted, along with the Merlin 24, a 400 gallon fuel tank was installed in the bomb bay for the ferry flight along with updated navigation, radar and radio equipment. These alterations set back the first flight of PA474 until August when it took off from Hawarden airfield, adjacent to the factory. The delay meant that the war in the Far East was also over and PA474 was surplus to requirements.

By the time it had landed at Llandow, South Wales it had only flown for a total of three hours and 10 minutes; here it was placed into storage with 38 Maintenance Unit where it remained for just over a year until it was moved to 32 MU based at St Athan in November 1946. It was saved from scrapping when it was selected to be used for photo mapping duties in East Africa. The conversion to PR.1 involved the installation of dual controls (still fitted), the removal and blanking of the turrets, a covered over cockpit roof and stripping of the paint back to

M 82 SQN, EAST AFRICA, 1948

a natural metal finish. A little over three years after it rolled off the production line PA474 finally entered service when it was received by 82 Squadron's B flight at RAF Benson on September 23, 1948. Given the code letter M and wearing the squadron crest on the nose, it was one of seven Lancaster PR.1s based at RAF Eastleigh, near Nairobi, Kenya. By 1952 the squadron had mapped over 1.2 million square miles and in February PA474 returned home.

Following an overhaul by Avro, PA474 was selected for conversion to a pilotless target drone with the work being done by Flight Refuelling Ltd, however it received a stay of execution when the conversion was cancelled by the Air Ministry. In lieu of Lancasters, two Lincolns and several Meteors were converted by the company and ended their careers being destroyed as target drones. PA474 was instead to be used as a flying testbed and operated by Cranfield College of Aeronautics, arriving there on March 7, 1954.

At Cranfield the markings remained unchanged but over the following decade some changes were made to PA474 with a view to it testing laminar flow wing forms for the next generation of transonic and supersonic jets in development. PA474 tested many wings during this period, including one intended for the Folland Midge and another produced by Handley Page.

For these flights a typical crew would consist of a pilot, flight engineer and two observers and two more from the Cranfield Flight Research team. The schedule was not taxing however and

AVRO LANCASTER B Mk.I PA474

M, LAMINAR FLOW WING FLYING TEST BED, CRANFIELD 1954

in just under 10 years PA474 only gained 100 flying hours. During this period most other surviving Lancasters were scrapped so the time at Cranwell may well have saved PA474.

The testing career was curtailed by the lack of spare Merlin engines and in October 1963 PA474 was passed on to the Ministry of Defence Air Historical Branch and was to become an exhibit at the planned RAF Museum. Still in post-war configuration it was flown to RAF Wroughton in April 1964 where 15 MU applied a typical bomber command scheme, albeit without any squadron codes.

In this new scheme it appeared in the film Operation Crossbow; still lacking turrets PA474 is easily identifiable. Stock footage of the Lancaster (with turrets) also appeared in the 1978 film Force 10 from Navarone, although many sources erroneously state it was The Guns of Navarone.

Later in the year, PA474 was transferred to RAF Henlow where exhibits for the new museum were being stored but due to the hangars being First World War types it had to be stored outside. A saviour appeared in the form of 44 Squadron's CO Wg Cdr Mike D'Arcy, who was after a Lancaster for Waddington, then operating the Vulcan. His officers scoured the country and eventually discovered there was a Lancaster at Henlow. The case was put forward that 44 Sqn was the first operational unit to be equipped with the Lancaster and at Waddington hangar space could be found to accommodate PA474.

The move was authorised and although the original intention was to chop it up and transport it by road, an inspection revealed that corrosion was minimal and PA474 was still airworthy, despite being exposed to the elements for a year. The only work required

OL-W 'JA928' TEMPORARY CODE FOR THE FILM OPERATION CROSSBOW, 1965

on the Merlins was the removal of a bird nest. Permission was eventually granted for one flight only, while avoiding built-up areas but on arrival over Lincoln several flypasts of the cathedral were made followed by beating up Scampton's main runway before landing at Waddington on August 18, 1965.

The original intention once at Waddington was for sufficient restoration work to be completed to stabilise the airframe for display but due to the excellent condition of PA474 the goal gradually shifted to one of eventually returning it to the air. Upon arrival it was given the markings of R5508 KM-B an original 44 Sqn Lancaster that had been flown by Sqn Ldr John Nettleton VC. On April 17, 1942, Nettleton was selected to lead the first of two waves on a daylight bombing raid to the Maschinenfabrik Augsburg Nürnberg AG diesel engine factory at Augsburg. The six Lancasters of 44 Sqn rendezvoused with six more from 97 Sqn, the latter forming the second wave, crossed the Channel at only 50ft and set course for Germany.

Most of the route had been cleared by nearly 800 fighters and some Bostons but near Beaumont le Roger airfield, Normandy, the attacking force was spotted by Luftwaffe Bf 109s and Fw 190s that had already intercepted RAF fighters and were returning to base. Only two of Nettleton's six Lancasters survived but the other plane, piloted by F/O J Garwell, was hit again over the target and crash-landed. Nettleton was gazetted on April 28.

Between PA474's arrival at Waddington and the start of 1967 a lot of work had been done to restore it to a wartime

KM-B 44 SQUADRON, WITH TURRETS FITTED, 1965

configuration with front and rear turrets fitted. A wood and fabric wind deflector for the rear turret was installed in 1985. The mid-upper was not fitted until 1976, the turret having been discovered in Argentina and brought back aboard the destroyer HMS *Hampshire*.

In 1967 Gp Capt Arthur Griffiths took over as station commander and took an interest in PA474. It was not long before he was convinced that it should fly again. Griffiths found much support from the upper echelons of the RAF, finally gaining financial support from the MoD. Permission for the work was then granted. Having not flown a Lancaster for 19 years, Griffiths re-familiarised himself with propeller aircraft during a one-hour trip in a Hastings. He then jumped in PA474 and took off on November 7, 1967 for an air test.

The following year PA474's first official display was at RAF Abingdon where it took part in a flypast during the Royal Review of the RAF during the 50 years celebrations on May 15, 1968. But the week before, on the 7th, it had made the trip to Jersey to participate in the 25th anniversary of the liberation of the Channel Islands. During the summer it flew in a total of 19 displays.

Demand for the Lancaster increased and it was soon flying for 50 hours per season. It was still being maintained by ground crew at Waddington but it became apparent that PA474 needed to be cared for long term and the logical solution was to transfer the Lancaster to the BBMF with which there was still the expertise and facilities to maintain the vintage aeroplanes. So on November 20, 1973 it became an official addition to the flight.

The move from Lincolnshire and Bomber County to Norfolk was

KM-F TEMPORARY FRENCH SCHEME FOR THE TV FILM LIEUTENANT KARL, MARCH 1976

not universally popular but in 1975 PA474 was granted the right to bear the city arms and since then it has, regardless of the scheme, always displayed the coat of arms and legend 'City of Lincoln' on the nose. PA474 and the BBMF soon returned to Bomber County, relocating to Coningsby on March 1, 1976, where it has since remained. As previously stated, the mid-upper turret was fitted later in the year and at the end of the 1979 display season a second representative scheme was applied. KM-B was replaced with those of Lancaster ED932, AJ-G, flown by Wg Cdr Guy Gibson during the Dambusters raid on the night of May 16/17, 1943.

Over the winter of 1983/84 the next major service took place at St Athan where the code was changed to SR-D, representing a Lancaster of 101 Squadron. Of all the Bomber Command squadrons that operated the Lancaster, 101 Sqn had the highest attrition rate with 1,176 crew lost. Four years later PA474 spent the winter at Exeter where West Country Air Services undertook the major servicing. Upon completion it was repainted in the markings of Lancaster ED888 PM-M2 of 103 Squadron for the 1988 season.

ED888 entered service with 103 Sqn in May 1943 with both 103 and 576 squadrons (returning to 103 Sqn in October 1944). During this time it flew a total of 140 operations, more than any other Lancaster, represented by the impressive mission tally on

KM-B 'CITY OF LINCOLN', REVISED SCHEME, 1976

the port side below the cockpit. After 50 ops it was awarded a DFC, upon reaching 100 ops it received a DSO, a bar was added to the DFC upon completion of the final 140th trip and these were also painted on the fuselage. Having survived the war, ED888 was ignominiously scrapped on January 8, 1947. PA474 returned to St Athan in late 1993 for another service, this time painted as WS-J W4964 of 9 Squadron, but more easily identified by the Johnnie Walker nose art and 'Still Going Strong' motto. W4964 had the distinction of being the last heavy bomber to complete 100 operations (106 in total). Further to this all the ops were with 9 Squadron and for the 100th mission it carried a 12,000lb Tallboy on one of the attempts to sink the *Tirpitz*.

For this particular raid the squadron, along with Lancasters of 617 Sqn, took off from Yagodnick, Russia on December 15, 1944. W4964 was the only one to record a hit and the damage inflicted resulted in the *Tirpitz* being moved conveniently 200 miles closer to the UK so the damage could be repaired. The illustrious career of W4964 also included flying on D-Day, multiple trips to Berlin, the shooting down of a Ju 88 and the destruction of a searchlight. Included with the bomb tally are the four DFMs and three DFCs won by crew members over the years and under each of these are their initials.

Unlike the other Lancasters PA474 has represented over the years, a section of W4964's mid-fuselage survived the chop and was, for several years, used as Ground Instruction Machine 4922M at 1 Air Armanent School, Manby. In 1949 it was no longer required, whereupon it

AJ-G 617 SQUADRON, REPRESENTING ED932, 1979

became a chicken coop in Gainsborough until it was rescued and placed on display at Newark Air Museum.

Two years after the last service and repaint, PA474 was once more back at St Athan in September 1995 for a major service. Due to fatigue on the airframe the decision was made in 1990 to replace the spar booms; this work had originally been intended for the previous service but postponed. At St Athan the Lancaster was dismantled and transported to BAE's Chadderton site where the work took place.

BAE created a custom jig to hold the centre section and inner wings, and the opportunity was also taken to replace other parts, including new Perspex to the mid-upper turret, wing joint shackles and some reskinning that was required due to minor corrosion. The replacement of the spars extended PA474's flying time by several thousand hours and it completed a successful test flight on May 13, 1996.

Unlike when it had gone in for services previously, PA474 did not receive a new scheme, instead it had to wait until 2000 when EE176 QR-M 'Mickey the Moocher' of 61 Sqn was the chosen aircraft, following yet another scheduled service at St Athan. EE176 was initially assigned to 7 Sqn on June 11, 1943, but within 10 days it had moved to 97 Sqn based nearby. The code started as OF-N but later changed to OF-O and it was used on multiple ops including 15 to Berlin until it was transferred to

AVRO LANCASTER B Mk.I PA474

SR-D 101 SQUADRON, 1984

61 Sqn at Syerston on November 20. The code was changed to QR-M, M for Mickey, so logically Mickey Mouse towing a bomb trolley was added as nose art and in a tribute to the popular song Minnie the Moocher EE176 was named 'Mickey the Moocher'. Over the next few months it was flown regularly by one crew and then another flying regularly over Germany and particularly Berlin. One raid stands out due to weather instead of enemy action. P/O J A Forrest RAAF and his crew took off for Nuremberg on March 30, 1944 but having dropped their bombs, EE176 was blown off course on the return leg and over the North Sea the Lancaster was hit by lightning.

The crew were stunned and Forrest was temporarily blinded, so believing they had already crossed the Norfolk coast he ordered the crew to bail out. Only Air Gunner H W Pronger and Wireless Operator Sgt L G Darben jumped. They were close but had yet to cross the coast so both landed in the sea and despite extensive searches they were never found.

EE176 went on to fly on D-Day and remained with 61 Sqn until it had completed its 128th op with a trip to Brunswick on the night of October 14/15, 1944. The war-weary Lancaster was sent to 1653 Conversion Unit and coded H4-X. It continued to fly until April 1945 when it became an instructional airframe.

PA474 continued to display regularly through the first few years of the 21st century until the end of the 2005 season when it yet again undertook a scheduled service and change of scheme. Staying with the

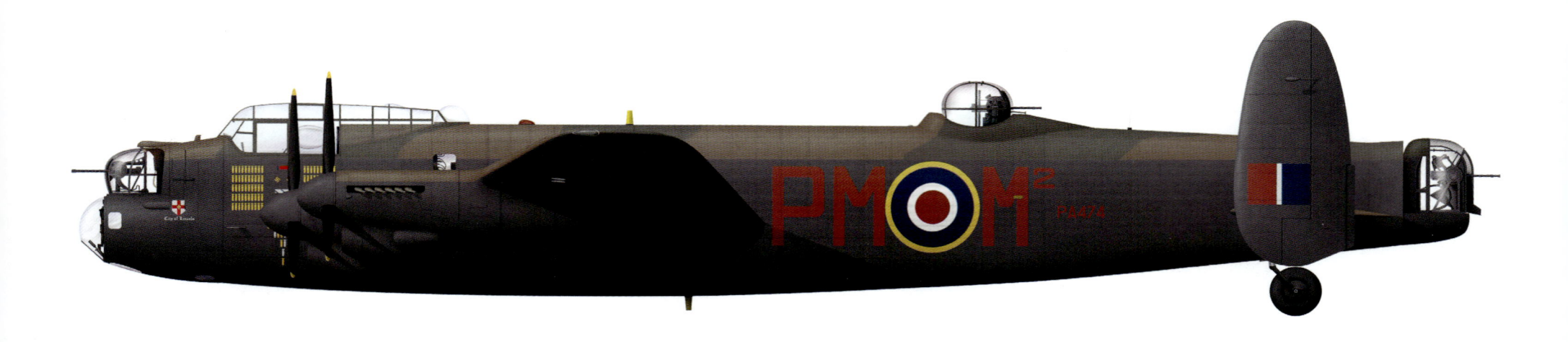

PM-M2 103 SQUADRON, REPRESENTING ED888, 1988

tradition of using the markings of one of the 35 Ton Up Lancasters (those that flew 100 or more missions), EE139 Phantom of the Ruhr was picked. PA474 wore 100 Squadron's code, HW-R on the port side and 550 Squadron's BQ-B on the starboard side along with the nose art of a phantom dropping bombs from a cloud. EE139 was chosen as the result of a chance encounter between BBMF crew and Flt Lt Ron Clarke, the first captain of EE139, who informed them that several of the original crew still survived. The scheme was unveiled for the 2006 display season.

The original EE139 was delivered to 100 Sqn at RAF Waltham at the end of May 1943 and allocated to Clark's crew. They took it for an air test on June 2 and a week later the fledgling crew and the new bomber took part in a raid on Dresden. Soon after this Flight Engineer Harold 'Ben' Bennett was tasked with creating nose art for EE139. He was given free reign and came up with the Phantom design. During the following months it flew a total of 33 ops while with 100 Sqn, with Clark as captain for 25 of those missions.

The crew's final trip in EE139 was on the night of September 23/24, 1943, when the target was the chemical works at Mannheim. Having dropped the bombs over the target they were coned (caught in multiple searchlights) and then attacked by an enemy fighter. They eventually got free at only 800ft but in the process the tail aileron had been damaged, causing vibrations. When the crew had safely landed they discovered the bomb bay had taken a direct hit from the flak. Following

WS-J 'JOHNNY WALKER' 9 SQUADRON, REPRESENTING W4964, 1994

the repairs, EE139 flew four more missions with the squadron before being transferred to a newly-reformed 550 Squadron at Waltham in November 1943. The code was changed to BQ-B and remained with the squadron for the next 12 months, adding to the number of ops and reaching an impressive 121 by the time it was retired from operational service in November 1944. It served briefly with a Heavy Conversion Unit but was scrapped in February 1946.

Following the service over the winter of 2005/2006 PA474 once again wore the markings of a 617 Sqn Lancaster, in a break from recent tradition the original only flew 50 missions, still an impressive total for a wartime bomber. Following the success of the dams raids the squadron replaced their heavily converted Lancasters for standard B.Is. Among the new aircraft was DV385, KC-A which arrived at Coningsby where the squadron had moved to in November 1943. DV385 was subsequently modified so the bomb bay could accommodate the massive Tallboy and Blockbuster bombs.

In January 1944, the squadron moved the short distance to Woodhall Spa where 619 Sqn was then based. It was here that the future captain of DV385 was already based; Robert 'Bob' Knights and his crew were coming up to complete their first tour of 30 ops with 619 Sqn and wanted to remain together, so they volunteered as a whole crew for a second tour with 617 Sqn.

Having originally flown his qualifying op as second pilot with the crew of EE112, which was T for Thumper and had the nose art on, Knights wanted to pay tribute to the crew of EE112 when it was lost on the night of August 10/11, 1943, so the aircraft was known as

QR-M 'MICKEY THE MOOCHER' 61 SQUADRON, REPRESENTING EE176, 2000

'Thumper Mk.II'. When Knights' crew transferred to 617 Sqn they were allocated DV385 and it naturally became 'Thumper Mk.III'.

DV385 went on to have a distinguished career during the war, being involved in Operation Taxable during which the bomber formation had to regularly drop window (small strips of foil) that would give the illusion of an invasion fleet sailing towards the Pas de Calais on D-Day. It also went on to drop several Tallboy bombs. A week later it was bombing the E-boat pens at Le Havre and then later in the year it was involved in two attacks on the Tirpitz with F/O James Castagnola as captain. Having survived the war, DV385 was officially struck off charge on November 11, 1946, and scrapped.

While flying as 'Phantom of the Ruhr' PA474 only had one minor but amusing incident when it required the assistance of the Luftwaffe. Engine number four went unserviceable at Schiphol Airport, Amsterdam, and the only available aircraft to fly a replacement Merlin from Coningsby was a Luftwaffe C-160. As 'Thumper Mk.III' there were more eventful moments. For the first time in several decades, PA474 was joined in the air by a second Lancaster when the Canadian-operated Mk.X FM213 flew across the Atlantic for the summer of 2014 and provided a highly popular draw for airshow crowds, on occasions also appearing with the Avro Vulcan XH558. Then, during a standard training flight on May 7, 2015, PA474 was forced to make an emergency landing, fortunately at Coningsby, due to a fire in

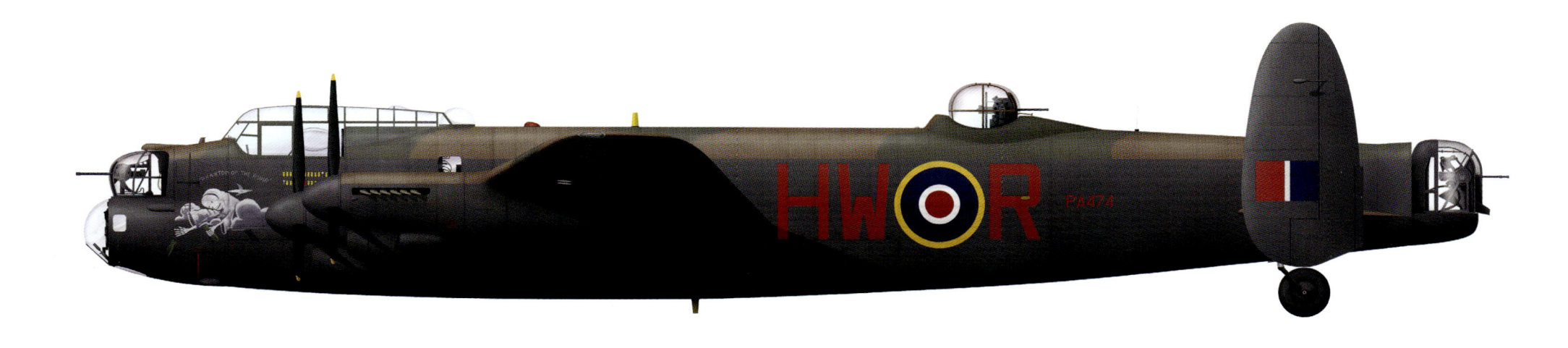

HW-R 'PHANTOM OF THE RUHR' 100 SQUADRON, REPRESENTING EE139 (STARBOARD SIDE EE139 BQ-B 550 SQUADRON) 2007

the number four (starboard outer) engine, caused by a misfire. The fire was suppressed, keeping damage to a minimum, but a rebuild was required and it undertook a test flight on October 12. The work was sufficient to see it through the 2016 season but at the end of the year it was delivered to the Aircraft Restoration Company, based at Duxford, for a scheduled major overhaul and the application of a new scheme following a complete repaint.

The starboard side was painted to represent LL922 VN-T of 50 Sqn, flown by Flying Officer Douglas Millikin DFC, a personal connection, as Douglas was the grandfather of the current BBMF OC, Sqn Ldr Andy 'Milli' Millikin. Of Douglas' ops 27 were in LL922 during the spring and summer of 1944. Not long after Millikin's crew last flew it was taken on a mission by Joe Palandri to bomb German troops in France and was shot down by a night fighter on the night of August 7/8. Four of the crew successfully bailed out and only one became a POW. Millikin went on to fly a second tour with 156 Pathfinder squadron.

For the port side another Lancaster with distinctive nose art was picked. W5005 AR-L did not have the honour of being a ton-up Lanc but it only narrowly missed out by a mere six ops. It was built in Manchester and delivered to 460 Sqn in May 1943, where it received the code AR-L (the code applied to PA474) and was allocated to the Australian Flt Sgt Ken Giles and his crew who flew only eight ops in it before their tour was complete.

460 Sqn was at this time a predominantly Australian unit. W5005 then became the personal aircraft of Sgt J D 'Jock' Ogilvie, one of the

KC-A 'THUMPER MKIII' 617 SQUADRON, REPRESENTING DV385, 2013

few Scots with the squadron. To reflect the mixed heritage of the crew they commissioned Fg Off Vic Watts, a navigator, to paint a bagpipe-playing kangaroo on the nose. Only black and white photos exist so there was some speculation on the colour of the tartan for the repaint.

Between late June and the end of July, Ogilvie's crew flew nine ops with the squadron CO Wg Cdr Martin taking W5005 for a couple of trips. It then passed to Jerry Bateman's crew who flew it on only their second op to Mannheim on August 9, 1943. By the time they had flown 23 ops they received a new Lancaster, ND394 AR-J2, and W5005 passed into the hands of Flt Sgt Cullen, by which time it had been re-coded AR-E2. Returning from its 51st trip W5005 almost overshot the runway and the starboard undercarriage collapsed.

Having been repaired it moved to 550 Sqn and became BQ-N although the nose art was retained and it went on to fly a further 43 missions with the squadron until returning from Kiel on the night of the August 26/27. It was badly damaged by flak and forced to ditch on the mudflats of the Humber Estuary. All the crew survived and made it to the shore but the 94th trip was to be the last for W5005.

Without D'Arcy and Griffiths' vision to preserve PA474 and restore it to flying condition the Lancaster may well have been just another museum exhibit collecting dust and there would be no flying tribute to all those who were lost or injured in the bomber campaigns of the war.

AVRO LANCASTER B Mk.I PA474

AR-L 'LEADER' 460 SQUADRON, REPRESENTING W5005, 2017

STARBOARD SIDE LL922 VN-T OF 50 SQUADRON, 2017

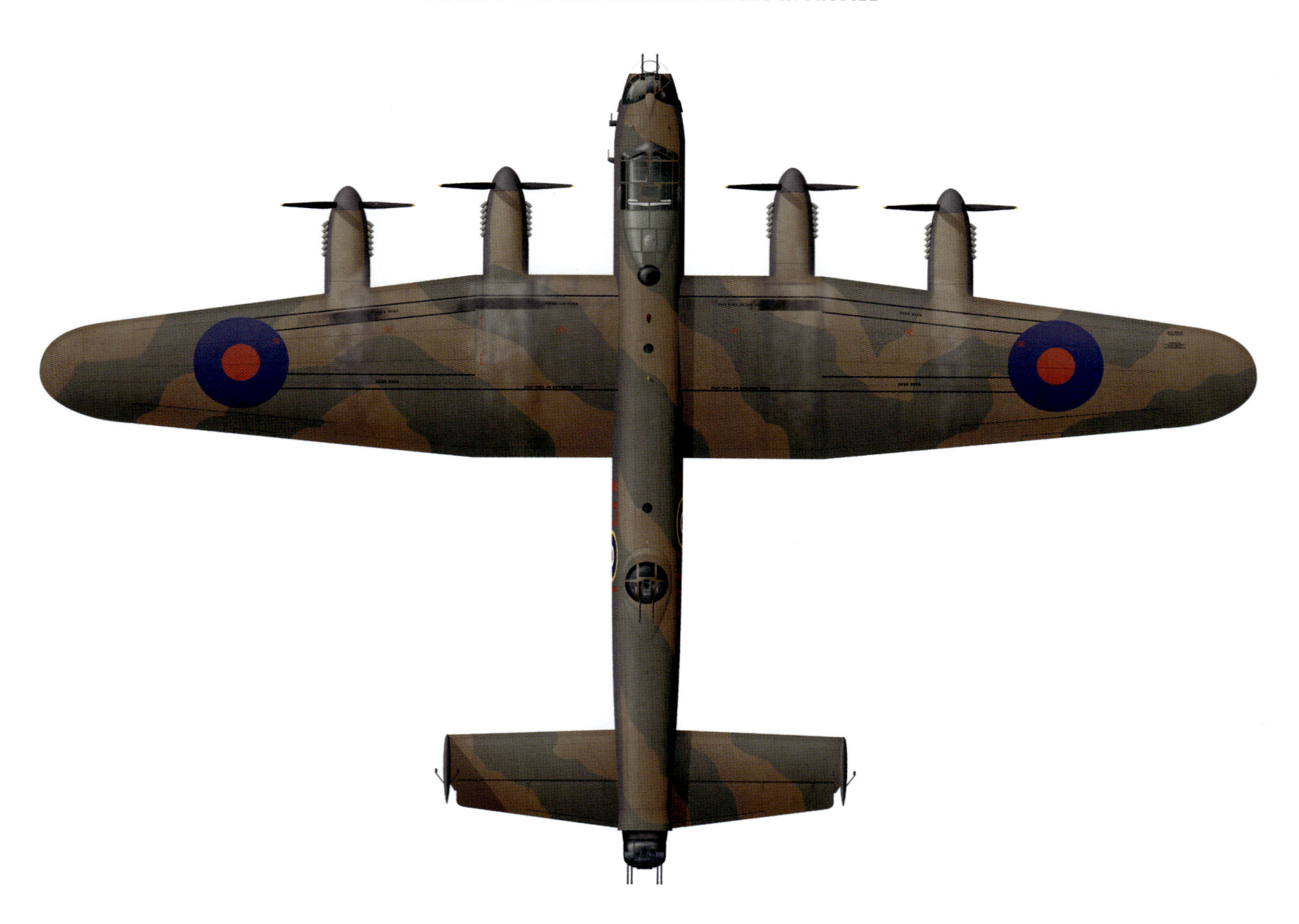

BATTLE OF BRITAIN MEMORIAL FLIGHT IN PROFILE

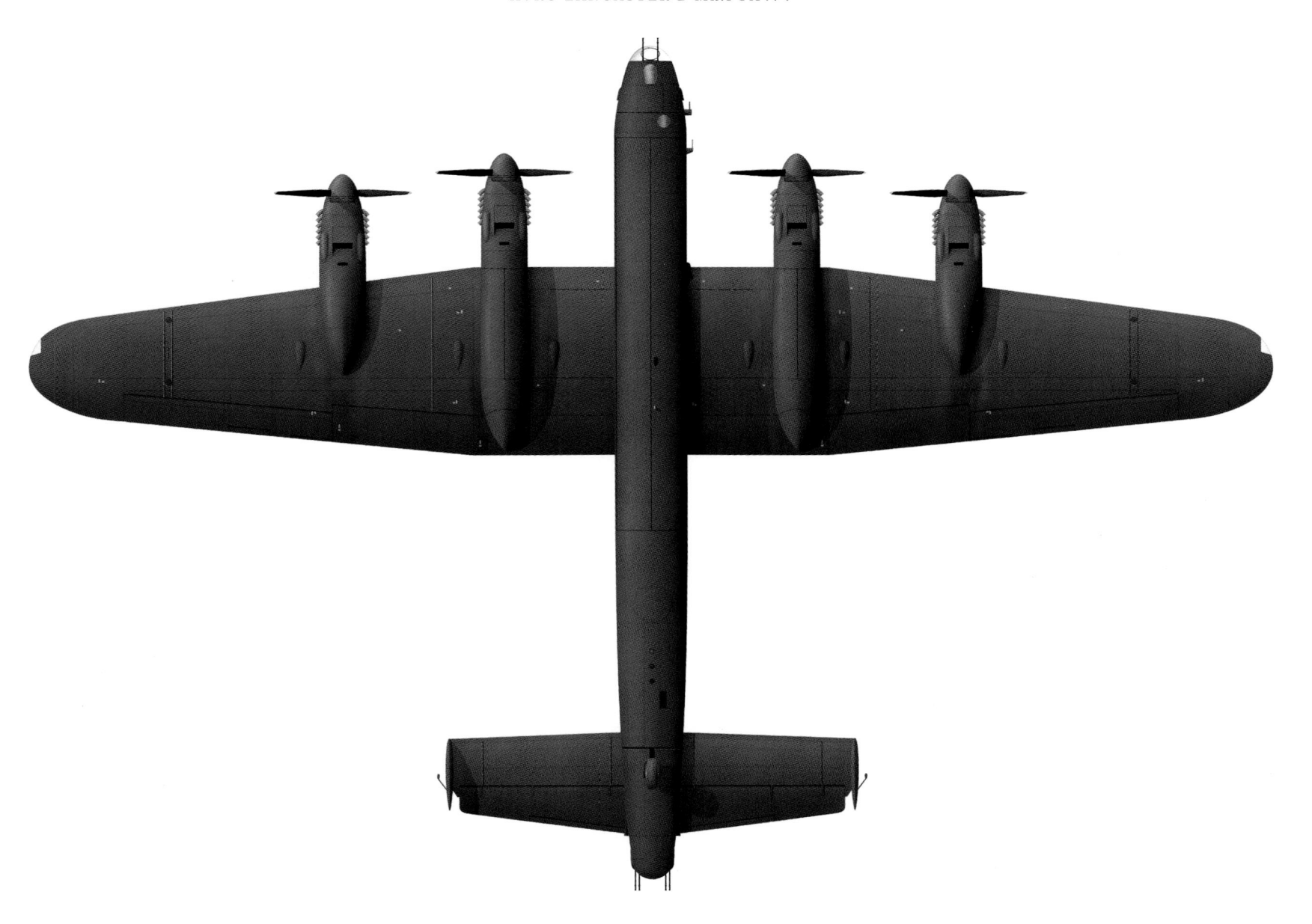

AVRO LANCASTER B Mk.I PA474

Photographed in the Lancaster PR.1 configuration while with 82 Squadron.
BBMF Archives

AVRO LANCASTER B Mk.I PA474

PA474 in a hangar upon return from mapping duties in East Africa with 82 Squadron. DAVID WELCH

The Lancaster was used for aerofoil testing with a variety of wing forms at Cranfield during the early 60s. TONY CLARKE

KM-B minus the mid upper turret at Coningsby during the 70s. JAMES KIGHTLY

Wearing the code of Gibson's dam buster Lancaster AJ-G during the early 80s. DAVID WELCH

The port side of PA474 as AJ-G of 617 Squadron. DAVID WELCH

PM-M2 with a Wessex in the background at Bruntingthorpe, July 18, 1993. ANDREW THOMAS

'Johnny Walker' WS-J making a pass. AD VERCRUIJSSE

En route to Blackpool for a display, QR-M 'Mickey the Moocher' on May 15, 2004. CROWN COPYRIGHT

AVRO LANCASTER B Mk.I PA474

PA474 making a pass over Derwent Water. CROWN COPYRIGHT

QR-M showing the 'City of Lincoln' badge on the starboard side.
AD VERCRUIJSSE

Three generations of Avro, the Lancaster, Shackleton and Vulcan.
JAMES KIGHTLY

PA474 being prepared for an engine test at Coningsby. CROWN COPYRIGHT

PA474 & RCAF Lancaster Mk.X FM213 in formation. ROB MONFEA

The Lancaster bomb bay. AUTHOR

'Phantom of the Ruhr' flying over Derwent Dam on the 65th anniversary of the Dambusters raid, June 16, 2008. CROWN COPYRIGHT

PA474 underwent a full overhaul during the winter of 2016/2017 at Duxford. AUTHOR

AVRO LANCASTER B Mk.I PA474

Close up of 'Leader' nose art. AUTHOR

View of the Lancaster cockpit. AUTHOR

Looking aft to the rear turret. AUTHOR

Touching down following a display at RIAT. ROB MONFEA

Three generations of 617 Squadron aircraft. ROB MONFEA

Flying in formation with Hurricane LF363 and Spitfire MK356. ERIN SANDHAM-BAILEY

Conducting a fly past during the Platinum Jubilee. LISA HARDING

ZA947 in formation with Hurricane PZ865 and Spitfire TE311.
LISA HARDING

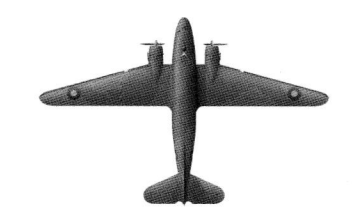

DOUGLAS C-47A DAKOTA ZA947

As well as being a display aircraft, the BBMF Dakota was originally taken on to act as a transport for supplies and crew when other aircraft were operating overnight away from Coningsby — and as a multi-engine tail dragger for use as a trainer while pilots converted to the Lancaster.

ZA947 was built as C-47A-60-DL at the Douglas Long Beach factory in 1942. The construction number was 10200 and it was originally allocated the serial 42-24338 at Long Beach.

ZA947 was officially delivered to the US Army Air Corps on September 7 but it was transferred to the Royal Canadian Air Force a week later on September 16 under the Lend-Lease Agreement and received the code 661.

As 661 it initially remained in Canada, serving with various units including 164 Squadron RCAF. During this time the crew added their names to the interior and these were uncovered during restoration and have been preserved by the BBMF.

In 1944 it was ferried to the UK to serve with 109 Communications Flight RCAF. During the early 1950s, 109 CF was based at RCAF Grostenquin, France. The base was also known as 2 (Fighter) Wing, which initially operated the Sabre and later the CF-100 and F-104. The flight operated a mix of aircraft including two Bristol Freighters, a Beechcraft C-45 Expeditor and four C-47s, including 661.

At some stage, probably the late 1950s, 661, along with all other RCAF Dakotas, lost its wartime paint and was finished in a white upper surface, natural metal lower fuselage with a light grey underside. Although no photographs are known to exist it is likely that the Canadian Red Ensign was worn as a fin flash along with a complex maple leaf roundel. Both the flag and maple leaf were revised and replaced on all military aircraft in 1965 so 661 would also have been repainted around this time. Following changes in French nuclear policy the RCAF left Grostenquin in 1964, relocating units around Europe with 109 CF ending up at Marville. The flight was later disbanded and 661 was surplus to requirements, being placed into storage at Prestwick.

The Royal Aircraft Establishment had been using a Dakota that was nearing the end of its flying hours and needed a

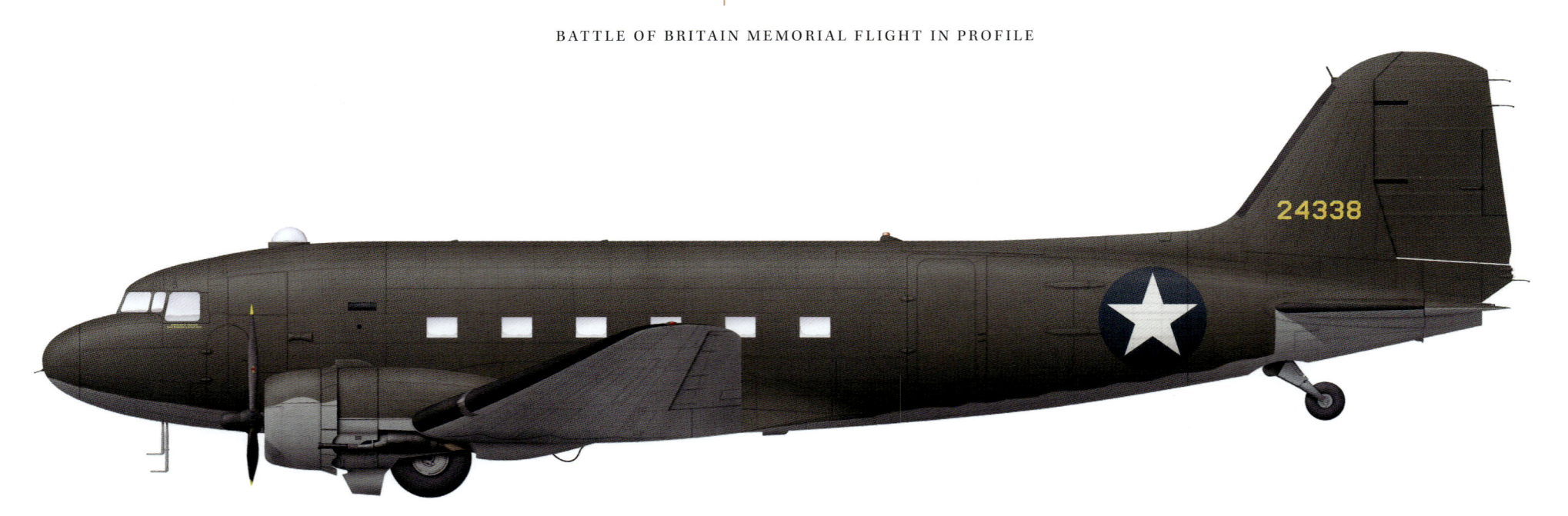

42-24338 USAAF FACTORY SCHEME, SEPTEMBER 1942

replacement, so 661 was acquired in April 1969 and given the serial KG661. It was incorrectly assumed at the time that this was the original serial.

Repainted in standard Transport Command colours and named 'Portpatrick Princess' it was allocated to the Electrical Quality Assurance Directorate (EQD) at RAF West Freugh along with C-47 TS423. Here it was used for a variety of testing roles including launching drones and sonobuoy batch testing, the latter requiring a hole to be cut in the lower fuselage for the purpose of dropping. Observation windows originally from a Canberra PR.9 were also installed in the lower fuselage. KG661 initially had the EQD crest on the tail with no fin flash and no text on the fuselage for a brief period when it was first in service

with the RAF. The crest was soon replaced with a fin flash and 'Royal Aircraft Establishment' was added to the upper fuselage.

There was concern over the accuracy of the serial KG661, with research revealing that the original C-47 KG661 had actually crashed at RAF Crosby, Cumberland, and been destroyed in a fire on December 13, 1944. In light of this information the serial ZA947 was allocated in July 1979 and has remained unchanged ever since. ZA947 continued being used for testing until it was transferred to Farnborough in 1982 and repainted in raspberry ripple. In 1985 ZA947 appeared at the International Air Tattoo wearing special markings to commemorate its appearance at the show and the 50th anniversary of the first flight of the DC-3 on December 17, 1935. The scheme was short-lived however.

CC-661 RCAF, SEPTEMBER 1942

The RAE's successor, the Defence Research Agency, decided that it no longer had a need for ZA947 and put it up for disposal in 1992.

It was acquired by Strike Command with a view to the BBMF using it as a replacement for the DH Devon as a support aircraft and crew transport. The pedigree of the type also better suited the BBMF than the post-war Devon. ZA947 underwent an overhaul with structural and engineering work being carried out by Air Atlantique at Coventry.

With the work completed in March 1993 it was ferried to RAF Marham and painted in an olive and green wartime scheme, representing YS-DM, KG374 of 271 Squadron flown by Flt Lt David Lord VC DFC during Operation Market Garden. Lord had joined the RAF in 1938 and was posted to his first operational squadron just before the outbreak of war, arriving at 31 Squadron in Lahore, India on October 7, 1939. The squadron began operating the Dakota in 1942. After several years abroad Lord returned to the UK in January 1944 and he was involved in D-Day operations, dropping paratroopers the night before the invasion in the Caen region.

Operation Market Garden was intended as a swift thrust into the Netherlands all the way to Arnhem with the intention of crossing the Rhine using an airborne assault. It was launched on September 17, 1944, and with a very stretched supply line the only way to resupply troops at the end was with air drops. 271 Sqn was tasked with the drop on September 19 and shortly after 1pm 17 C-47s took off from RAF Down Ampney.

At Arnhem the fighting was fierce with the German forces being supported by flak batteries. As Lord was approaching the drop zone,

CC-661 109 COMMUNICATION FLIGHT RCAF, RED ENSIGN FIN FLASH, 1958

KG374 was hit in the starboard engine. Lord continued to fly straight and level while the crew dropped the supplies, however two containers still remained so, despite the fire spreading, Lord returned for a second run. This time the wing came off and the Dakota crashed. The only survivor was the navigator, Flt Lt Harold King, who was thrown clear and had time to deploy his parachute. King joined up with paratroopers of the 10th Battalion, Parachute Regiment and became a prisoner of war. It was only upon repatriation that he could report on Lord's actions and he was gazetted in November 1945.

ZA947 was not to suffer being relegated to only secondary roles however. It was an active participant on the display circuit and undertook many paratrooper drops, the most significant of these was in 1994 when ZA947 was the first to make a drop during the 50th anniversary of Operation Overlord over Ranville near Pegasus Bridge. Later in the year it returned to the continent and was involved in the 50th anniversary events commemorating Operation Market Garden.

Air Atlantique was once more responsible for servicing ZA947 at the end of the 1997 display season and the opportunity was taken to apply a new scheme, albeit one very similar to the previous one. The colours and paratrooper badge remained just behind the forward crew door and YS was retained, but this time it was YS-H of 77 Squadron. 271 Sqn had been renumbered as

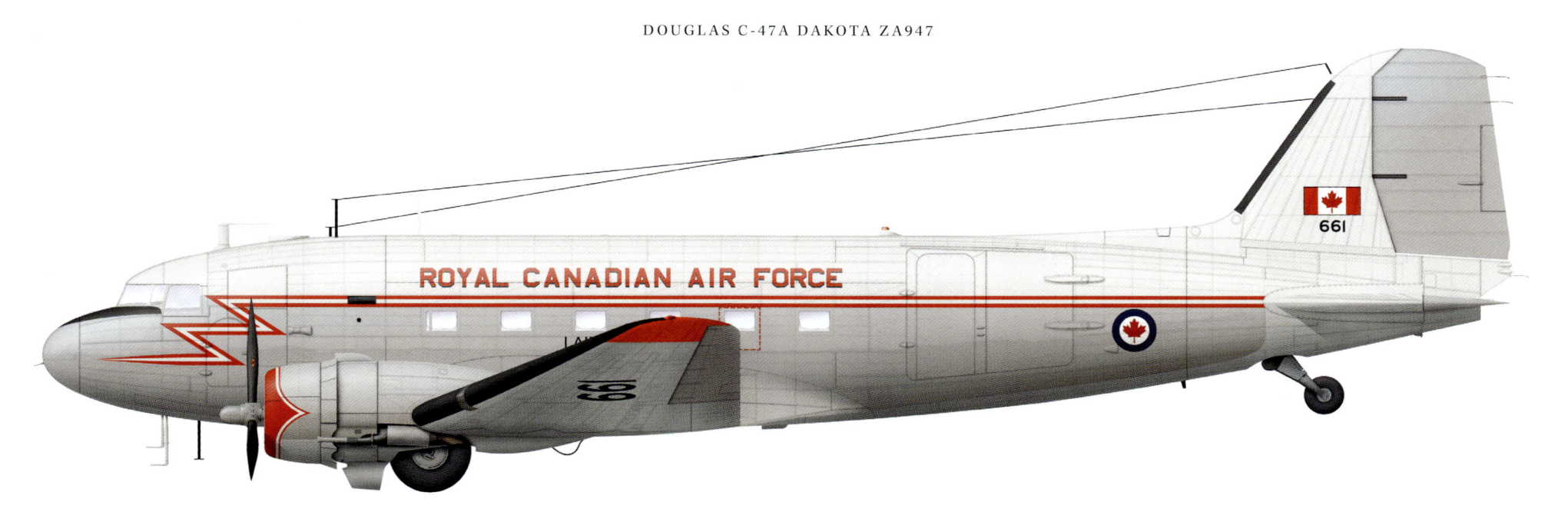

CC-661 109 COMMUNICATION FLIGHT RCAF, CANADIAN FLAG FIN FLASH, 1965

77 Sqn and the squadron code letters had been retained (the previous 77 Sqn had been renumbered as 31 Sqn in November 1946 in India). The style of the letters altered, with the YS being in white instead of red. The scheme was chosen to coincide with the 50th anniversary of the Berlin Airlift (in 1999) which 77 Sqn had been heavily involved in, being based at RAF Fassberg, Germany, at the time.

A camouflage scheme was introduced in 2003 and 267 'Pegasus' Squadron was chosen as the source for the scheme. It was based on those worn while the squadron were based at Bari, Italy, during 1944. The squadron operated in the Middle East and Mediterranean for the majority of the war, first in Egypt and following the invasion of Italy flying resupply missions to partisans in Greece and Yugoslavia.

The squadron also supported resistance fighters in Poland during Operation Wildhorn, an attempt to recover V-2 parts for inspection. The squadron was posted to India in February 1945 to support the Burma campaign. Although a variety of camouflage was worn during the war, all squadron aircraft wore a Pegasus on the nose. ZA947 was the subject of major work in 2004 when the modifications made during its time with the RAE were undone and the cabin was restored to the original wartime standard with paraseats and the hook-up wire fitted along with authentic flooring. Having worn the same scheme for eight years, ZA947 was repainted in 2011 to represent FZ692, Kwicherbichen (named by her crew) of 233 Squadron which was involved in para-dropping the night before D-Day and resupplying

KG661 'PORTPATRICK PRINCESS', ROYAL AIRCRAFT ESTABLISHMENT, 1979

troops in the following days. Once forward landing sites had been established the squadron undertook casualty evacuation flights and between June and the end of December the unit flew 1,092 stretcher wounded and a further 467 sitting wounded.

Further interior restoration followed the 2015 season with an authentic period colour used to repaint the instrument panels and interior, while preserving the writing made by wartime crews. Casualty stretchers were installed and the instrument panels, flight instruments and interior floor were removed for inspection. ZA947 continues to be the workhorse of the BBMF while being a flying tribute to the often overlooked aircraft and crews who flew in the less glamorous but at times just as dangerous transport and supply role.

The Dakota was absent for the duration of the 2023 season as it undertook another thorough service conducted by Aircraft Restoration Company at Duxford. Upon completion it was decided that ZA947 would wear South East Asia Command roundels for the first time when it represented FD781 of 31 squadron which operated from India and Burma. The original FD781 was delivered to the USAAF on January 27, 1943 with the BuNo 42-5657 and subsequently transferred to the RAF who allocated the new code and delivered it on April 1, 1943 to 31 Squadron based in India. It remained with the RAF until it was returned to the USAAF 10th Air Force (also in India) on October 26 1944.

When FD781 was first handed over the standard RAF

ZA947, 'PORTPATRICK PRINCESS', ROYAL AIRCRAFT ESTABLISHMENT, 1980

markings were applied with type C.1 roundels, to avoid confusion with the Japanese Hinomaru, the red centre was painted over. The original intention was for ZA947 to wear this style of roundel but the later SEAC version where the pale blue replaced the white was selected.

31 Squadron was formed in 1915 and soon dispatched to the North-West Frontier in what was then the British Indian Empire and remained in the region until 1947. By the time of the Japanese invasion of Burma (Myanmar) the squadron was fully equipped with the C-47 and began flying support and supply missions. During the Japanese advance one C-47 evacuated a total of 65 individuals which included refugees, walking wounded and the crews of two other Dakotas which had been lost. As the war progressed the Dakotas regularly flew over the Himalayas which came to be known as 'the Hump' by the pilots. Many of these missions were to drop supplies to the Chindits who were operating deep behind enemy lines. While most deliveries were by parachute, the C-47s were known to land in jungle clearings. In once such trip known as the 'Piccadilly Incident' Sqn Ldr Mike Vlasto DFC & Bar flew FD781 150 miles behind the Japanese front line into and out of a naturally formed 800 yard long and 400 yard wide clearing a mere 14 miles from a Japanese airfield near Bhamo in Myanmar, the aim being to extract 18 wounded Chindits, led by Major Walter Purcell Scott.

It is the first time that the BBMF has paid tribute to the aircrews who flew regularly in dangerous conditions through the Himalayas and Far East, providing lifesaving support to the soldiers in the jungles.

BATTLE OF BRITAIN MEMORIAL FLIGHT IN PROFILE

RASPBERRY RIPPLE RAE SCHEME, 1982

INTERNATIONAL AIR TATTOO/DC-3 50TH ANNIVERSARY SCHEME, 1985

DOUGLAS C-47A DAKOTA ZA947

YS-DM 271 SQUADRON, REPRESENTING KG374, 1993

YS-H 77 SQUADRON, BERLIN AIR LIFT, 1998

BATTLE OF BRITAIN MEMORIAL FLIGHT IN PROFILE

AI 267 'PEGASUS' SQUADRON, 2003

'KWICHERBICHEN', 223 SQUADRON, REPRESENTING FZ692, 2011

DOUGLAS C-47A DAKOTA ZA947

31 SQUADRON SOUTH EAST ASIA COMMAND 2024

BATTLE OF BRITAIN MEMORIAL FLIGHT IN PROFILE

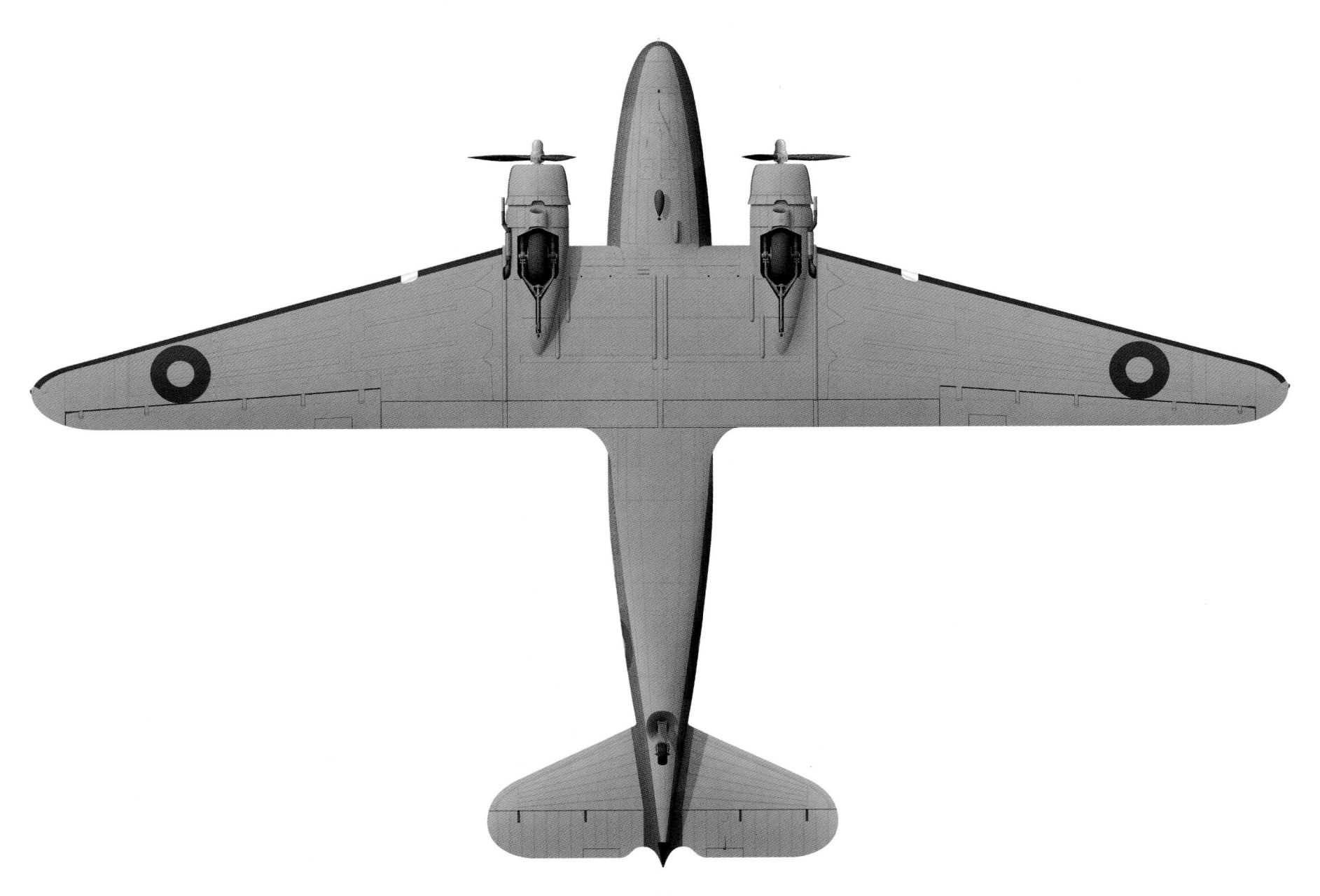

DOUGLAS C-47A DAKOTA ZA947

A rare image of 661 in wartime service with the RCAF, January 1947.
BBMF ARCHIVES

661 in 109 Communication Flight markings, photographed during a stopover at Gatwick in 1966. KEITH BURTON

KG661 in transport command colours at West Freugh in March 1977.
IAIN C. MACKAY

ZA947 photographed during a visit to Gütersloh in October 1982.
WILFRIED ZETSCHE/SG-ETUO.DE

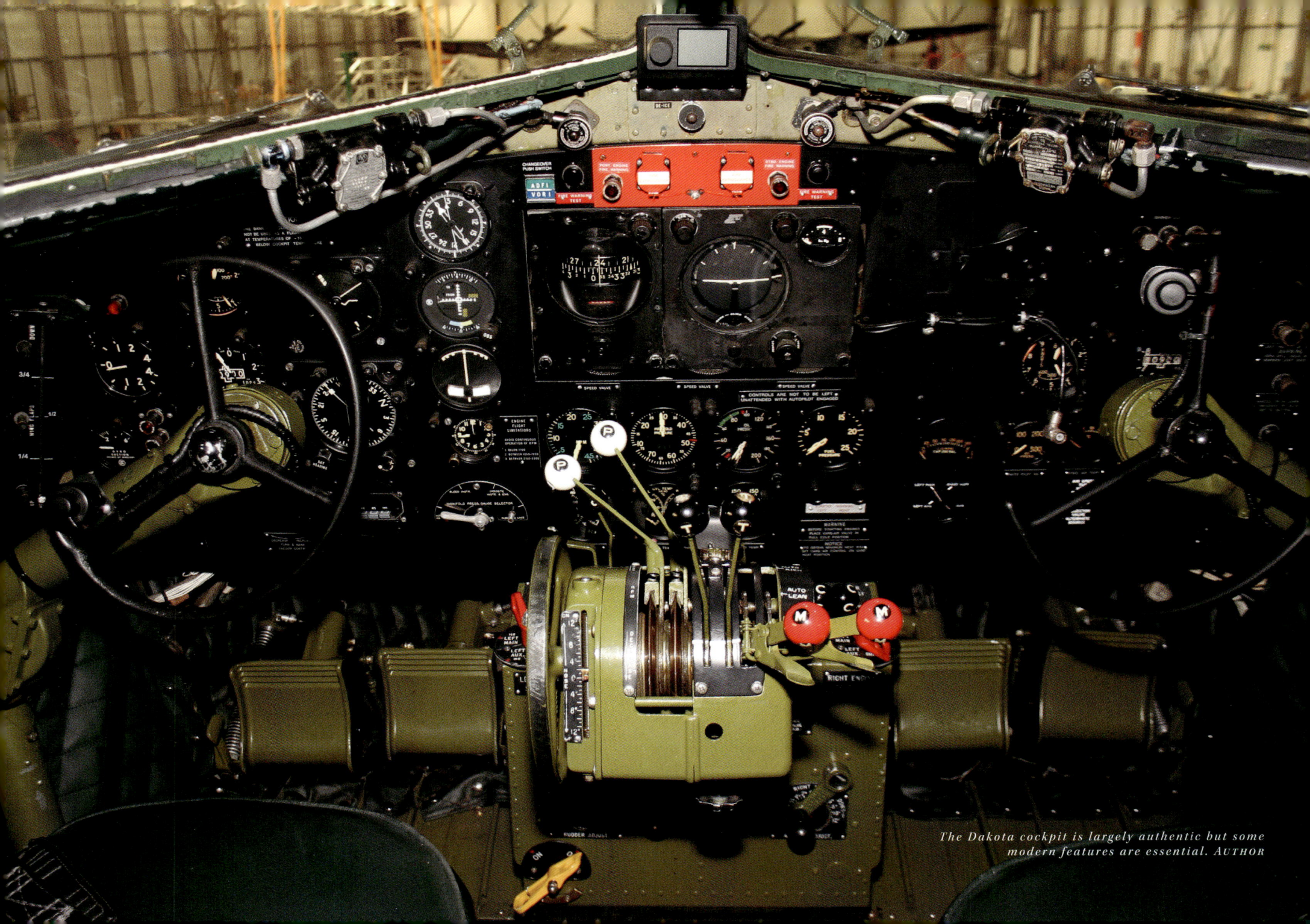

The Dakota cockpit is largely authentic but some modern features are essential. AUTHOR

ZA947 in 267 Squadron markings, waiting to take off at Duxford.
RONNIE OLSTHOORN

DOUGLAS C-47A DAKOTA ZA947

The distinctive Raspberry Ripple markings of RAE aircraft. IAN GRATTON

Another view of ZA947 showing underwing detail at Gütersloh in October 1983. WILFRIED ZETSCHE/SG-ETUO.DE

While painted as YS-H the Transport Command crest was worn on the starboard side. ANDREW THOMAS

ZA947 undergoing engine maintenance at Coningsby. JAMES KIGHTLY

In formation with Hurricane PZ865 and Spitfire AB910.
RONNIE OLSTHOORN

Wearing D-Day markings the Dakota in the process of taking off for a display in April 2015. CROWN

Conducting a fly past over Coningsby provides a good view of the underside of ZA947. LISA HARDING

The restored interior of ZA947 looking towards the cockpit. AUTHOR

An evening takeoff at Coningsby. LISA HARDING

2021 witnessed the 75th anniversary of the Chipmunk and an opportunity for the BBMF pair to take centre stage at Old Warden, it being rare for them to both appear at displays. AUTHOR

DE HAVILLAND DHC-1 CHIPMUNK WG486 & WK518

It is somewhat fitting that the BBMF continues to operate the last two of 735 Chipmunks in RAF service as the aircraft was used to train thousands of pilots on tail dragger types since it was first introduced to the University Air Squadrons in 1950.

Once all RAF single engine aircraft were tail draggers but with the advent of the jet age even propeller-powered aircraft began to use the nose wheel configuration. As such, the skills required to handle a Spitfire or Hurricane on the ground have long been in decline.

In order to prepare plots converting from fast jets to its Second World War veterans, the BBMF keeps two Chipmunk T.10s on strength. De Havilland Canada had been building the ubiquitous Tiger Moth under licence during the war and deemed it time to employ advances in aviation to construct a monoplane successor for basic flight training. The Chipmunk first flew on May 22, 1946, only eight months after the first designs were created, and entered service with the RCAF the same year.

The RAF expressed an interest and arranged for its orders to be constructed in the UK with the first production Chipmunks delivered to Oxford University Air Squadron in February 1950. They went on to serve with the Reserve Flying Squadrons, RAF Volunteer Reserve and later provide Air Experience Flights to Air Cadets until 1996 when they were eventually retired in favour of the Scottish Aviation Bulldog.

The first of the two Chipmunks flown by the fight was handed over in 1983 and is still used regularly to prepare pilots for conversion to Spitfires and Hurricanes. WK518 was built at the de Havilland factory at Hawarden, Broughton (the same factory where the Lancaster PA474 had been built seven years earlier) and taken on by the RAF on January 29, 1952. It was then sent to the RAF College at Cranwell.

During the next few years it moved around considerably, serving with Liverpool UAS, Manchester UAS, Cottesmore Station Flight in 1958, Cambridge UAS, Hull UAS 1960-1966,

WG486 114 SQUADRON, CYPRUS, 1958

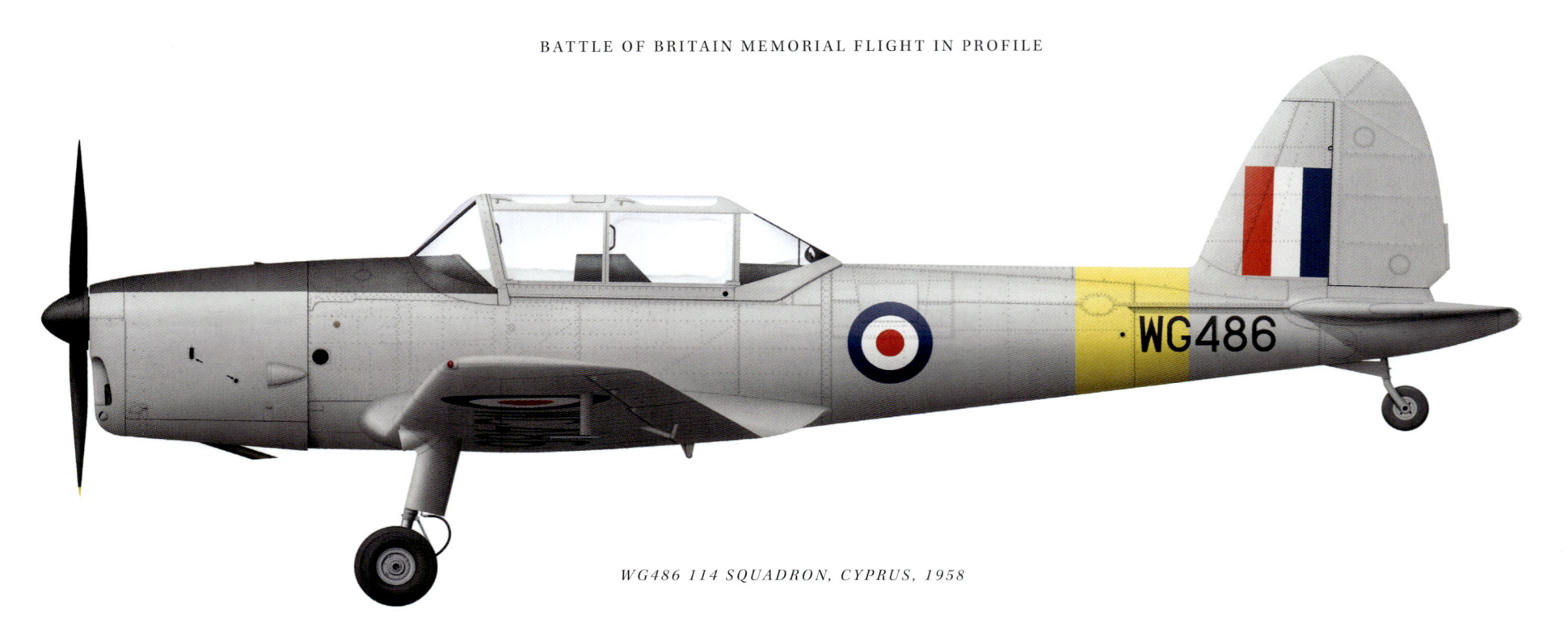

Leeds UAS 1966-1969 and London UAS 1969-1974. At the latter, it was repainted in Light Aircraft Grey with Dayglo stripes and 1 Air Experience Flight where it received the red and white scheme.

In April 1983 it was delivered to the BBMF and had 'Battle of Britain Memorial Flight' applied just below the canopy on both sides. It remained in this scheme until 1994 when it was painted in the original scheme of Silver with Oxford and Cranwell Blue bands on the rear fuselage.

This lasted until 2000 when both of the BBMF Chipmunks were painted in all over gloss black, as were all RAF trainer aircraft. It reverted to the Hull UAS markings in 2012 and wore them until 2020 when it once again wore the London UAS scheme.

WG486 was also built at Hawarden and delivered to the RAF on January 3, 1952. It was finished in an all over silver scheme and the following month it was sent to 5 Basic Flying Training School at Desford, Leicestershire, where it remained until July 1953 when the base was closed.

WG486 was then transferred to 9 Refresher Flying School, Doncaster, until the unit was disbanded on February 16, 1955. 2 Flight Training School at Hullavington was the next destination and the Chipmunk stayed there until it was purloined by the Army, serving with 651 and then 657 Squadron Army Air Corps when it was re-formed on September 1, 1957.

This secondment only lasted a year as it was pressed into

WG486 114 SQUADRON WITH CODE LETTER AND REPAINTED SPINNER, CYPRUS, 1958

operational service with 114 Squadron the following year. It was transported to Cyprus as part of Operation Thwart during the crisis leading up to independence at the end of the 50s when the EOKA guerrilla organisation was targeting British forces. Arriving in December 1958, Chipmunks were involved in convoy escorts and low level reconnaissance, usually with an Army officer in the rear seat.

WG486 returned to the UK once operations ceased in March 1959. Initially it was based at Cranwell, followed by 1 Initial Training School, South Cerney, Gloucestershire, and later Church Fenton. The Chipmunk then moved to Linton-on-Ouse where it joined 1 Flying Training School. Next was a period with Liverpool UAS. In 1967 trainers including the Chipmunks were painted in Light Aircraft Grey with Dayglo stripes added and then in 1972 it was transferred to Bristol UAS, which retained it for just a year. Remaining at Filton, WG486 was officially operated by 3 Air Experience Flight and repainted in a red and white scheme.

The scheme changed once more when WG486 was again called upon for operational duties, this time undertaking observation and photographic reconnaissance over Soviet-controlled Berlin and East Germany.

WG486 arrived at Gatow in the British sector of the city during May 1987 and was returned to the all over Light Aircraft Grey scheme. The Chipmunk flights were arranged by the British Commanders-in-Chief Mission to the Soviet Forces in Germany (BRIXMIS) and although the flights were sanctioned by the Soviets the Flight Notification Cards

WG486 LIVERPOOL UNIVERSITY AIR SQUADRON, 1961

were stamped 'Safety of Flight Not Guaranteed'. Indeed on more than one occasion a Chipmunk returned with extra holes although no one was ever injured during these flights.

With the fall of the Berlin wall, unification and withdrawal of Soviet forces there was no further need for spy flights but the Chipmunk remained stationed at Gatow until 1994 when it moved to Laarbruch, Germany, and became part of the station flight. No longer required in Germany, WG486 was handed to the BBMF so the flight once again had two Chipmunks on strength.

Previously WP855 had been with the flight until it went to 1AEF in 1987. WG486 retained the Light Aircraft Grey scheme until it was painted in standard RAF trainer all over black in 2000. In keeping with the rest of the aircraft operated by the flight, WG486 was repainted for the 2018 season in the markings of Bristol UAS, which it had previously worn in the early 70s.

Designed as trainers for the RAF the two Chipmunks have continued the tradition of training pilots albeit in a slightly different role now, both were present for a special event at Old Warden celebrating the 75 years the type first flew. The BBMF Chimpunks days are sadly numbered due to the increasing costs and reduction in availability of parts so as nice as it would be for the BBMF to continue flying the trainers, the Chipmunks fall outside the core BBMF remit and replacements will eventually be sought.

DE HAVILLAND DHC-1 CHIPMUNK WG486 & WK518

WG486 BRISTOL UNIVERSITY AIR SQUADRON, 1972

WG486 3 AIR EXPERIENCE FLIGHT, 1973

BATTLE OF BRITAIN MEMORIAL FLIGHT IN PROFILE

WG486 8 AIR EXPERIENCE FLIGHT & GATOW, GERMANY, 1987

WG486 RAF TRAINER GLOSS BLACK 2000

DE HAVILLAND DHC-1 CHIPMUNK WG486 & WK518

WG486 BRISTOL UNIVERSITY AIR SQUADRON

*WG486 BRISTOL UNIVERSITY AIR SQUADRON
WITH 2021 REPLACEMENT COWLING*

BATTLE OF BRITAIN MEMORIAL FLIGHT IN PROFILE

DE HAVILLAND DHC-1 CHIPMUNK WG486 & WK518

BATTLE OF BRITAIN MEMORIAL FLIGHT IN PROFILE

WK518 CRANWELL, 1952 & 1994

WK518 HULL UNIVERSITY AIR SQUADRON DURING 1960 & 2012

DE HAVILLAND DHC-1 CHIPMUNK WG486 & WK518

WK518 UNIVERSITY OF LONDON AIR SQUADRON, 1969

WK518 UNIVERSITY OF LONDON AIR SQUADRON, 1970

BATTLE OF BRITAIN MEMORIAL FLIGHT IN PROFILE

WK518 1 AIR EXPERIENCE FLIGHT, 1974. JOINED BBMF 1983

WK518 RAF TRAINER GLOSS BLACK, 2000

DE HAVILLAND DHC-1 CHIPMUNK WG486 & WK518

WK518 UNIVERSITY OF LONDON AIR SQUADRON 2020

WK518 UNIVERSITY OF LONDON AIR SQUADRON 2020

BATTLE OF BRITAIN MEMORIAL FLIGHT IN PROFILE

DE HAVILLAND DHC-1 CHIPMUNK WG486 & WK518

BATTLE OF BRITAIN MEMORIAL FLIGHT IN PROFILE

WG486 whilst with 114 Sqn based in Cyprus during 1959.
DAVE WELCH

Photographed at Cottesmore in September 1973, WG486 was flown by Bristol UAS at the time. ROBIN WALKER

Shortly before being transferred to Germany WG486 was at Shawbury in May 1987. MIKE DOWSING

While undertaking spy flights over East Germany WG486 was based at Gatow but also flew from Berlin Tempehoff during the late 1980s.
BRUCE WILLIAMSON/SPYFLIGHT.CO.UK

286

DE HAVILLAND DHC-1 CHIPMUNK WG486 & WK518

Detail of WG486 tail with the BBMF crest, WK518 in the background. CROWN COPYRIGHT

Following the fall of the Berlin Wall officers of the 6th Guards Independent Motor Rivle Brigade, Karlshorts, East Berlin inspected the spy planes during a visit to RAF Gatow. LAWRENCE SKUSE

WG486 undergoing engine maintenance at Coningsby.
JAMES KIGHTLY

WG486 showing the all over gloss black trainer scheme worn from 2000.
KEITH WILSON

Undertaking an air test in March 2018 the Bristol UAS scheme.
TONY CLARKE

DE HAVILLAND DHC-1 CHIPMUNK WG486 & WK518

An excellent photo showing the Dayglo markings on the upper surfaces of WG486. TONY CLARKE

The nose cowling on WG486 retained the AEF red and white for many months as this detailed photo taken during servicing in the BBMF hangar shows. AUTHOR

Ground crew conducting tests on WG486 at Coningsby in August 2020. LISA HARDING

WG486 being prepared for the flight home from Old Warden as rain clouds gather. AUTHOR

Displaying the original Hull UAS scheme worn by WK518, taken at Waddington in September 1961. KEN ELLIOT

WK518 retained the 1 Air Experience Flight scheme when it first arrived at Coningsby in 1983. CROWN COPYRIGHT

The two BBMF Chipmunks flying in formation over Lincolnshire. KEITH WILSON

WK518 being refuelled at Coningsby following a flight in February 2015. CROWN COPYRIGHT

WK518 undergoing routine maintenance at Coningsby in December 2017. AUTHOR

DE HAVILLAND DHC-1 CHIPMUNK WG486 & WK518

WG486 & WK518 in formation. AUTHOR

Taxiing past ZA947. CROWN COPYRIGHT

Waiting in the hangar while PZ865 is prepared for an engine test. AUTHOR

WK518 being refuelled at Shuttleworth ready for a flight home. AUTHOR

Coming in to land while an 11 Squadron Typhoon waits to take off. TREV HURLEY

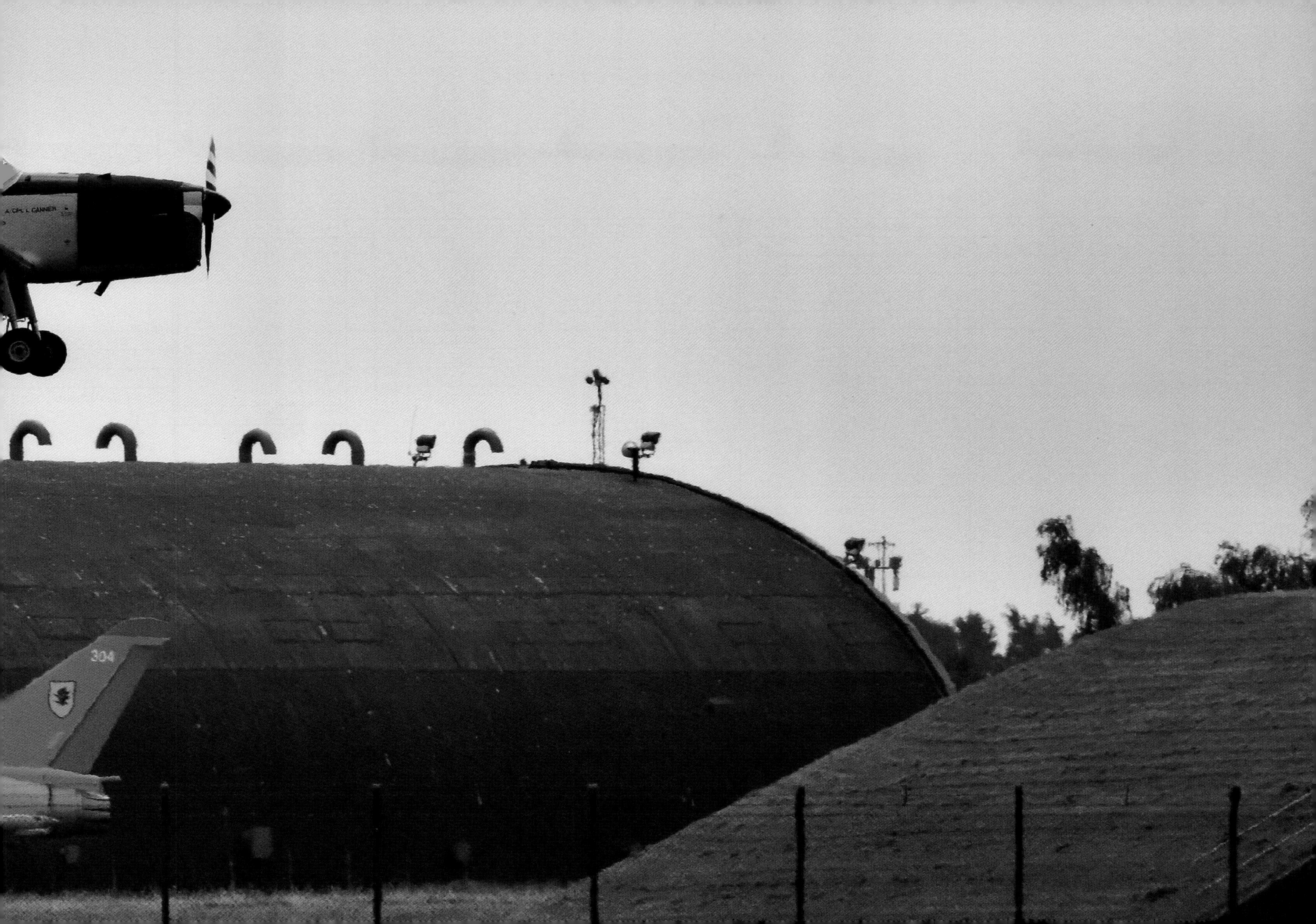
304

	SPITFIRE IIA P7350	SPITFIRE VB AB910	SPITFIRE LFIXE MK356	SPITFIRE XVIE TE311	SPITFIRE PRXIX PM631	SPITFIRE PRXIX PS915
1940	UO-T 226 Sqn/XT-W 603 Sqn					
1941	QJ- 616 Sqn/SH-D 64 Sqn	ZD-C 222 Sqn/PJ- 130 Sqn				
1942	Central Gunnery School	MD-E 133 Sqn/LE- 242 Sqn				
1943	57 OTU	DN- 416 Sqn				
1944	Unknown Code	AE-H 402 Sqn	2I-V 443 Sqn			
1945	Storage	53 OTU	5690M	Empire Central		514 Squadron
1946		WT-S 527 Sqn	Halton	Flying School		No Code
1947		G-AISU	Instructional Airframe	33 MU		
1948	RAF Colerne Collection			Storage		K-OI 2 Sqn
1949					226 OCU	
1950					Unknown Code	
1951			Hawkinge	Flying Training Command		
1952			Gate Guardian	Ferry Training Unit		
1953						
1954		Vickers		2 Civilian AA	THUM Flight	THUM Flight
1955				Tangmere		
1956				Gate Guardian		
1957					Historic Aircraft Flight	West Malling
1958		QJ-J			No Codes	Gate Guardian
1959		92 Squadron				
1960		(Vickers)				
1961			Bicester Gate Guardian			Leuchars
1962			Locking			Gate Guardian
1963			Gate Guardian			
1964						
1965						
1966						

APPENDIX

HURRICANE IIC LF363	HURRICANE IIC PZ865	LANCASTER I PA474	DAKOTA III ZA947	CHIPMUNK T.10 WG486	CHIPMUNK T.10 WK518	
						1940
						1941
			42-24338 USAAF/CC-661 RCAF			1942
			CC-661			1943
63 Sqn, WC-F 309 Sqn, RM- 26 Sqn	Last of the Many		RCAF			1944
62 OCU	Hawker	38 MU Storage				1945
Unknown Code		32 MU Storage				1946
Thorney Island						1947
Station Flight		M				1948
		82 Squadron				1949
Flying Training Command	G-AMAU King's Cup					1950
Angels One Five film	US-B Angels One Five film					1951
Flying Training Command	G-AMAU Last of the Many			5 Basic Flying Training School	RAF College Cranwell	1952
	Hawker			9 Refresher Flying School		1953
		M				1954
Reach for the Sky film		Cranfield		2 Flying Training School	Liverpool/Manchester UAS	1955
Flying Training Command					Cambridge/Hull UAS	1956
Historic Aircraft Flight				651 Sqn/657 Sqn	RAF Lichfield	1957
No Codes			CC-661	114 Sqn	RAF Cottesmore Stn Flt	1958
			109 CF			1959
			RCAF	Cranwell/	Hull UAS	1960
				1 Initial Training School/		1961
				1 Flying Training School		1962
						1963
						1964
		KM-B				1965
		44 Squadron			Leeds/Hull UAS	1966

BATTLE OF BRITAIN MEMORIAL FLIGHT IN PROFILE

	SPITFIRE IIA P7350	SPITFIRE VB AB910	SPITFIRE LFIXE MK356	SPITFIRE XVIE TE311	SPITFIRE PRXIX PM631	SPITFIRE PRXIX PS915
1967					AD-C	Leuchars
1968	Battle of Britain film*	Battle of Britain film*	Battle of Britain film*	Battle of Britain film*	Battle of Britain film*	Gate Guardian
1969	ZH-T	SO-T	RAF Museum	RAF Exhibition Flight	AD-C	
1970	226 (Rhodesia) Squadron	145 Squadron	Reserve Collection		11 Squadron	
1971						
1972	UO-T	QJ-J				
1973	226 (Rhodesia) Squadron	92 Squadron				
1974						
1975						Bawdy
1976						Gate Guardian
1977						Coningsby
1978	QV-B	Grounded (Accident)				St Athan
1979	19 Squadron					Gate Guardian
1980						Bawdy
1981		XT-M				Gate Guardian
1982	SH-D	603 Squadron				
1983	64 Squadron					
1984					DL-E	Restoration
1985	EB-Z				91 Squadron	BAe
1986	41 Squadron	BP-O				
1987	(Observer Corps)	457 Squadron RAAF				No Codes
1988						
1989	UO-T					
1990	226 (Rhodesia) Squadron	EB-J 41 Squadron		QV-I	N 'Mary'	
1991	YT-F	MD-E		19 Squadron	11 Squadron (SEAC)	
1992	65 (East India) Squadron	133 (Eagle Squadron	St Athan			Yellow P
1993			Restoration			

* Wore multiple codes during filming

298

APPENDIX

HURRICANE IIC LF363	HURRICANE IIC PZ865	LANCASTER I PA474	DAKOTA III ZA947	CHIPMUNK T.10 WG486	CHIPMUNK T.10 WK518	
Historic Aircraft Flight	Hawker	KM-B 44 Squadron	CC-661 109 CF RCAF	Liverpool UAS	Leeds/Hull UAS	1967
Battle of Britain film*	Battle of Britain film*					1968
No Codes	G-AMAU Last of the Many				London UAS	1969
LE-D 242 Squadron	Hawker					1970
						1971
	DT-A 527 Squadron			Bristol UAS 3 Air Experience Flight		1972
						1973
					1 Air Experience Flight	1974
						1975
						1976
						1977
						1978
GN-F 249 Squadron	JU-Q 111 Squadron	AJ-G 617 Squadron	KG661 RAE			1979
						1980
			ZA947 RAE			1981
	Last of the Many					1982
VX-Y 85 Squadron		SR-D 101 Squadron			BBMF	1983
						1984
						1985
						1986
NV-L 79 Squadron	RF-U 303 Squadron	PM-M2 103 Squadron		BRIXMIS Gatow, Germany		1987
						1988
						1989
GN-A 249 Squadron						1990
						1991
Grounded (Accident)	J 261 Squadron		YS-DM 271 Squadron			1992
						1993

	SPITFIRE IIA P7350	SPITFIRE VB AB910	SPITFIRE LFIXE MK356	SPITFIRE XVIE TE311	SPITFIRE PRXIX PM631	SPITFIRE PRXIX PS915
1994	RN-S 'Enniskillen' 72 Squadron	AE-H 402 Squadron RCAF	St Athan Restoration	QV-I 19 Squadron	N 'Mary' 11 Squadron (SEAC)	Yellow P
1995						
1996					S 681 Squadron (SEAC)	
1997	BA-Y 'The Old Lady' 227 Squadron	ZD-C* 222 (Natal) Squadron	2I-V 443 Squadron RCAF			
1998				LZ-V 66 Squadron		UM-G 152 Squadron (SEAC)
1999	XT-D 'Blue Peter' 603 Squadron					
2000						
2001						
2002				Restoration	No Code 541 Squadron D-Day Stripes	
2003		IR-G 244 Wing				
2004						'The Last' 81 Squadron
2005						
2006	XT-W May only					
2007	XT-L 603 Squadron	RF-D 303 Squadron				
2008						
2009	QJ-K 92 Squadron		UF-Q 601 (County of London) Squadron			
2010						
2011	EB-G 41 Squadron				No Code 541 Squadron	
2012		MD-E/Refurbishment		4D-V 74 Squadron		
2013						
2014		SH-F 'PeterJohn' 64 Squadron	5J-K 'Kay' 126 Squadron		No Code 541 Squadron D-Day Stripes	
2015						
2016						No Code, Refurbishment
2017	QJ-G Port/QV-A Stb		QJ-3 92 Squadron	Black		
2018	KL-B 'KIWI III' 54 Squadron			SZ-G 316 Squadron		
2019						
2020						
2021						
2022					Refurbishment	
2023		AE-H 402 Sqn		3W-M/322 Squadron	Historic Aircraft Flight	

APPENDIX

HURRICANE IIC LF363	HURRICANE IIC PZ865	LANCASTER I PA474	DAKOTA III ZA947	CHIPMUNK T.10 WG486	CHIPMUNK T.10 WK518	
Grounded (Accident)	J 261 Squadron	WS-J 'Johnnie Walker' 9 Squadron	YS-DM 271 Squadron	Laarbruch, Germany	BBMF Cranwell	1994
				BBMF Light Grey		1995
						1996
						1997
US-C 56 Squadron	Q 5 Squadron		YS-H 77 Squadron			1998
						1999
		QR-M 'Mickey the Moocher' 112 Squadron		Gloss Black	Gloss Black	2000
						2001
			AI 267 Squadron			2002
						2003
						2004
YB-W 17 Squadron	JX-E 1 Squadron					2005
						2006
		HW-R 'Phantom of the Ruhr' 100 Squadron				2007
						2008
						2009
						2010
						2011
	EG-S 34 Squadron		'Kwicherbichen' 223 Squadron		Hull UAS	2012
						2013
JX-B 1 Squadron		KC-A 'Thumper' 617 Squadron				2014
						2015
						2016
GN-F/SD-A 249 Sqn/501 Sqn		AR-L/VN-T 'Leader' 460 Squadron/ 50 Squadron		Bristol UAS		2017
						2018
						2019
	ZY-V 247 Squadron				London UAS	2020
						2021
RJ-F 303 Squadron						2022
			31 Squadron			2023

301

BATTLE OF BRITAIN MEMORIAL FLIGHT IN PROFILE

1977-1981
Sqn Ldr Ken 'Jacko' Jackson

1981-1984
Sqn Ldr C S 'Scott' M Anderson

1984-1987
Sqn Ldr Tony Banfield

1987-1991
Sqn Ldr Colin Paterson

1992-1994
Sqn Ldr Andy Tomalin

1994-1996
Sqn Ldr Rick Groombridge

1996-2003
Sqn Ldr Paul 'Major' Day

2004-2006
Sqn Ldr Clive Rowley

2006-2009
Sqn Ldr Al Pinner

2009-2012
Sqn Ldr Ian 'Smithy' Smith

2012-2015
Sqn Ldr Duncan 'Dunc' Mason

2015-2018
Sqn Ldr Andy 'Milli' Millikin

2018-2022
Sqn Ldr Mark 'Disco' Discombe

2022-2025
Sqn Ldr Mark 'Suggs' Sugden

2025-2027
Sqn Ldr Mark Long

APPENDIX

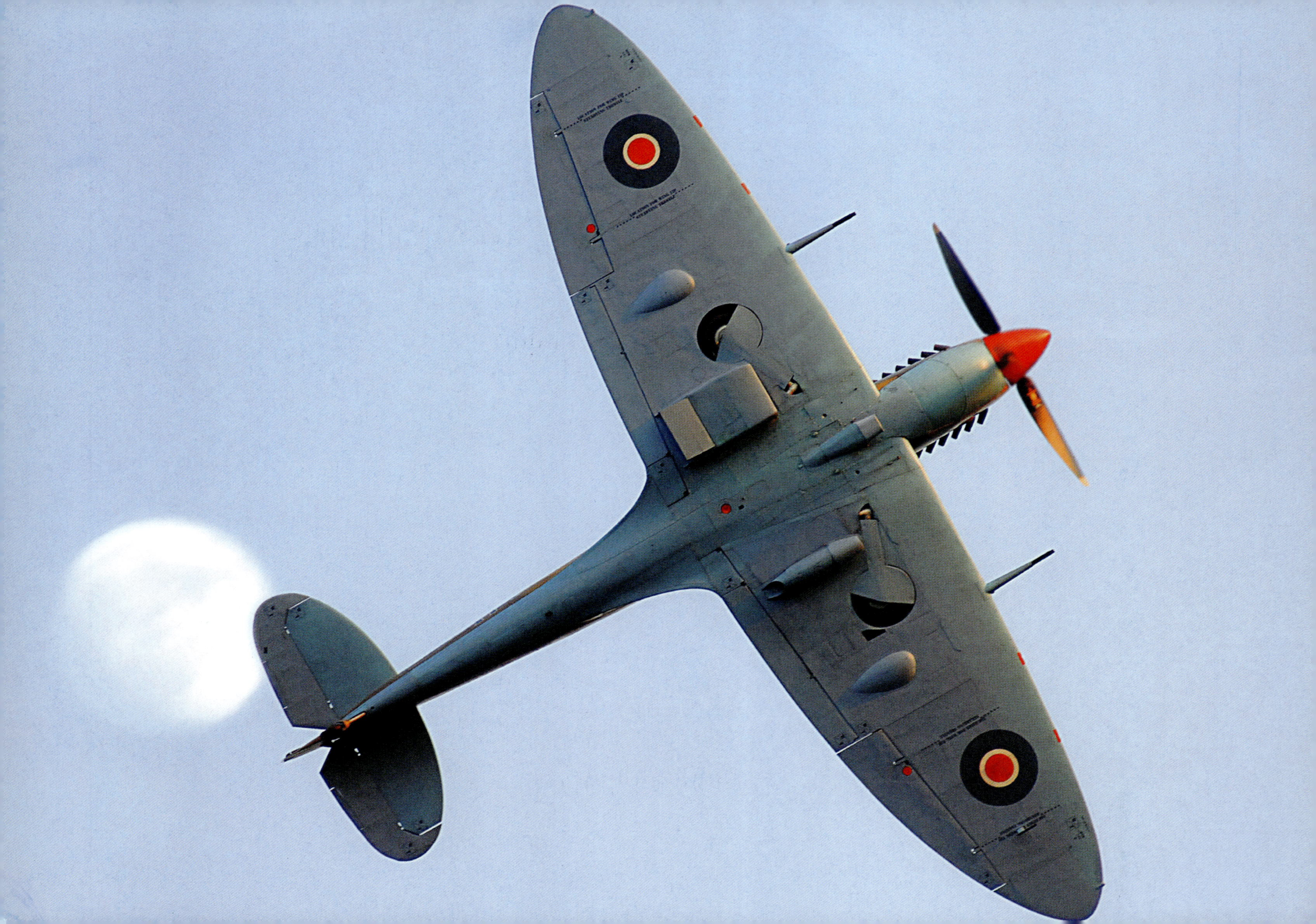